HEY, BY GEORGE!

George W. Denn

T o all of my ancestors those hardy pioneers that helped carved this nation out of a wilderness. Those that Lived before my time! Also to all of those who I new and loved. To my nephews and nieces, and all the young men that have helped me run this farm over the years. For you represent the future! To the Robert Smesrud family That own, and have rented the farm to my family for 45 years now! To you all I dedicate this book.

Acts chapter 17 verses 24-31

"The God who made the world and every thing in it is the Lord of heaven and earth and does not live in temples built by hands. And he is not served by human hands, as if he needed anything, because he himself gives all men life and breath and everything else. >From one man he made every nation of men, that they should inhabit the whole earth; and he determined the times set for them and the exact places where they should live. God did this so that men would seek him and perhaps reach out for him and find him, though he is not far from each one of us. 'For in him we live and move and have our being.' As some of your own poets have said, 'We are his offspring.' Therefore since we are God's offspring, we should not think that the divine being is like gold or silver or stone-an image made by mans design and skill. In the past God over looked such ignorance, but now he commands all people everywhere to repent. For he has set a day when he will judge the world with justice by the man he has appointed. He has given proof of this to all men by raising him from the dead."

George's Home circa 1976

The stories in this book are from real-life experiences I've had, as well as from some of the people I've come in contact with on my everyday work on the farm God has put me on since my birth on April 20, 1962, and in my spiritual walk with my Lord and Savior, Jesus Christ. These stories are in chronological order commencing in March of 2000. It is my sincerest hope that these stories will help strengthen your faith or perhaps bring you into a personal relationship with Jesus Christ. I would also like to encourage you to share your stories with others. May God bless all of you who read this book! Peace and blessings to you all!

Your friend in Christ,

George Denn

March 31, 2000

—∞∞∞—

The last week in February and the first week in March were unusually warm this year and fields were drying out faster than I was ready for. Instead of getting machinery ready, I was cutting up a tree between two neighboring houses as a fundraiser for the Eagle Lake Church of Christ. I wanted to get this done before fieldwork started. You cannot serve both God and money, I figured. So, I finished the tree on Sunday afternoon with a lot of unexpected help!

I started fieldwork on Tuesday, March 7th. What a beautiful day! I started planting oats on the 8th. It was a little rainy at first, but it cleared up after a while. Sure takes long enough to get things lined up! By 10:30 am Dad showed up so I drove to Mankato to sign up for a farm program. Sure wish I could just do one thing at a time. I pray for God to bless my time.

Wednesday it rained — where did the nice weather go? Half done with a field and I get rained out. I just hate that! On Thursday cold weather returned. Is the ground frozen hard enough to plant on top of the frost? Does that even work?? At least I've got that field done. I'll start another field after church on Saturday and then again before church on Sunday. Once I'm at church, someone there says it's snowing hard, so it looks like I'm done again! Next morning, the snow is frozen but the ground is dry underneath; who ever heard of planting in the snow?!

Sometimes I think I must be out of my mind to do this kind of work, but time will tell! By 8:30 the sun had gotten too warm and I had to quit, figuring I would have to wait till tomorrow, but then it froze again. No matter – I started at 6 am and then once again had to quit by 8:30. This is taking forever! As the tractor goes back and forth across the field, I remember the Parable of the Sower (Matthew 13). After a week of planting oats, I finally finish! How is it all going to turn out? Guess we'll just have to wait and see. Friday, March 17th — Time to start planting wheat. Saturday March 18th — snowing again! But I plant anyway until noon. I think this is a wild spring! On Monday it is too wet. Looks like it'll have to be done Tuesday, but isn't that Care meeting day?

Someone stops by at 9:30 Monday evening and doesn't leave until 1:30am. Wants to argue about Scripture, but I'm pretty stubborn about what I believe, and this person even says so! Tuesday another person stops at 11:30 am to buy meat and doesn't leave till 2 pm. I wonder where these people were last winter when I had no planting to do? As I'm planting I see sea gulls flying overhead so close I can see their eyes, and I think of how God cares for the birds of the air and how He cares for each one of us.

Ran out of seed at 5:30 on Thursday, with four acres still left to plant. I drive home in the rain, wondering, *don't I lead worship on Saturday? Need to pick out songs.* Friday it rains; Saturday I finish planting wheat after church services, and also I got to talk with a friend about Christ on Saturday evening. Told him to read John 3. How will the seeds turn out that we have been sowing? Only God knows!

Your friend in Christ,
George Denn

June 15, 2000

———— ❧ ————

My all-time favorite scripture from the Old Testament is **Ecclesiastes 11:1-2**: *Cast your bread upon the waters, for after many days you will find it again. Give portions to seven, yes to eight, for you do not know what disaster may come upon the land.*

Recently I was able to experience this scripture first hand. As most of you know, my main crop is hay. What a beautiful first crop it was to be, and I had buyers for all of it and then some. My 90 acres of Alfalfa hay was worth about $15,000, which I needed to cover bills and expenses that come with general farming procedures.

People I do business with pretty much know that when I get paid, they get paid. Before I started putting up hay this year I asked God to bless things, but most of all that the hay crop would glorify Him.

For those of you who aren't familiar, there is a small window of time for hay to be put up, baled, or chopped to be useful as livestock feed, and rain on hay is about as welcome to me as a computer virus is to those of you who work on them every day. So, ninety acres of hay that has been cut for two weeks and then rained on for as long is basically worthless as livestock feed. So that means saying goodbye to my $15,000 earnings! But for some reason I can't say goodbye to my bills that I owe other people. In other words, this stacks up to be a test! And I do mean a TEST! But I believe as a Christian you must be flexible, and to become flexible you must be stretched! I wonder where God is in all of this and I pray about it continually, but I don't seem to be getting the answers I want to hear, and furthermore, any attempt to come up with a solution pretty much fails. I prayed to

God to give me a solution to all of this because if He didn't, my checkbook would be overdrawn to the tune of $1,700 and I really didn't relish the idea of explaining the reasoning for this to all the people I owed. Besides, I am not too sure they would care. Most of them are out on a limb doing business with me in the first place — at least that is what some have said, to put it mildly!

I believe God has given me an idea for the damaged hay, because only He can make something good come out of something that is damaged, kind of like what Jesus did for us on the cross. But in the meantime I need to live. I called a longtime hay buyer of mine to see if he might be interested in some of last year's hay at a reasonable price. I prayed about this before I called him, and he said he might be interested. Praise the Lord! He wasn't 100 percent sure he could use it, but he told me he wanted to give me $2,500 whether he took the hay or not because he remembered a time three years ago when he owed me $16,000 and couldn't pay me for about three months. I remembered all that and how I had trusted him, and I believed Jesus would have trusted him also. You know that saying, what would Jesus do? It's the Christian way. Well, he paid me then. I remembered I was happy to get paid, contrary to the popular belief of most people at the time who thought he would never pay me. He said to me, "You trusted me then and I have never forgotten that!" So praise God, he generously leaves $2,500 with me since he knows he'll need more hay sometime anyway, and now my checking account has been salvaged.

As I close this writing, I want to repeat **Ecclesiastes 11:1-2**: *Cast your bread upon the waters, for after many days you will find it again. Give portions to seven, yes to eight, for you do not know what disaster may come upon the land.*

How about this, my readers: have you ever tried casting your bread upon the waters? If you haven't, don't you think it is time you did?

Your friend in Christ,
George Denn

October 20, 2000

—⸻—

When I started writing this book, I wanted to write about my everyday experiences with the Lord and also of other people I knew. At this time I'm going to pass the limelight to my friend and brother in Christ, Tony Foty. This is a poem he wrote to his wife Vickie, and he shared this with me the other day. With this being the harvest season, I thought it was fitting and proper to share it with all of you.

Joy of His Harvest
(Foty Family Harvest Prayer)
Only by His grace
We can sow His seeds together, you and I.
Only by His will God will provide rain and snow.
We show them the way,
Provide them some space in a place
That always is warm and safe.
We teach them how to know the weeds from the wealth,
And to keep out the weeds that will attempt
To keep His light from shining all about them.
We know that our workday is full,
So we take up His yoke knowing that we have
Been given all the tools we will ever need
to do what is to be done.
We watch as the season becomes rough,
And through His words and our prayers we are
Able to brace what is planted against the

Winds that will pull so many from their anchor.
We forgive the ones that try to trample
What we have planted, knowing the Father is
Keeping watch, for there will be others that
Care not what is under foot.
We sing this new song about His love to lead others
To what we have found in His harvest; He loves us
Even though we have failed and are not worthy.
We give thanks and gather in His name.
It's time to send His little ones out to remove the fruit
From the vines and bring in the reward.
We share in His love,
Break bread, drink wine,
In memory of His gift to all of us,
The gift of life, His son, Jesus.
He sows these seeds together with you and I,
So that when they are not so little they will also know
The way to sow the seeds of joy and be part of
His bountiful harvest forever.

~~~Tony Foty

Thanks to Tony for sharing this heartfelt poem with us all. Let us all remember our part in the spiritual harvest of which Jesus Christ our Savior has called us to be a part.

Your friend in Christ,
George Denn

November 10, 2000

———∞———

On November 5th I was listening to my friend Jeff preach a sermon to his congregation about Nehemiah - specifically, the prayer in Nehemiah chapter 1. My mind started to wander (does anyone else out there have that problem?); I often wonder about spiritual things in an earthly way. Later Jeff said he was greatly encouraged by the way my face looked as I listened to his sermon. I had to tell him that what I really had been thinking about were ideas for this book, but not that Jeff's sermon was boring, because it had been far from that! But rather, his sermon was inspiring me. Anyway, during the sermon I thought of Nehemiah and how he was in charge of rebuilding the walls around Jerusalem. He had started out as a cupbearer to the king, who was in exile, and had ended up being appointed governor in the land of Judah. My mind wandered back in time to a period of restoration in my own life.I've got this patch of land that's a little over an acre in size down along the lake that used to be my old cow yard. After I had quit keeping cows for milk, this piece of land had become overgrown with weeds, tree stumps, years and years of barbed wire fencing, some buried in the dirt, some poking up here and there all along the old fence line. It became kind of an old, abandoned, messy area that looked a lot like my life before my Christian conversion. I had only been a Christian for a short time when I decided to restore this section of my farm into something that could be productive.

I had a young man helping me at the time. We dug around all the stumps and sawed them off. We covered what was left of them with dirt, and pulled up the barbed wire. We worked at the weeds until finally they were all mowed down or pulled out. This whole process took probably a month to complete. At the time neither Ryan nor I would have ever thought that at some point I would be writing about the restoration of this piece of land. Thinking back on the work involved reminds me of a new Christian. God works in a person's life to remove the overgrown weeds and debris, cleaning them up and straightening them out so that they can begin to live productively for the kingdom of God.

But beware! Sometimes there are stumps below the surface that need time to rot before you can do any deep tillage in that area! In my mind these areas represent hidden sins, something we all deal with.

We did this work on my property five years ago, and this past year I thought that it sure would be nice to plow that area, so I did in preparation for planting corn. To my surprise, some of the stumps had completely rotted and were now mixed into the soil. Three or four were partially rotted, and the plow easily ripped the remaining roots, so that I could remove them with the loader. But some of the stumps were still hard, and when the plow bottom hit them they just tripped it.

This is how it is with the sins in our lives: some rot pretty quickly and are gone, some are a little tougher and get brutally ripped out, exposed for all to see, and some are almost as strong as ever. The only thing that we can do with the sins in our lives is to give them directly to our Lord and Savior Jesus Christ and let His blood cover them and eventually rot them away. That is why He died on the cross, you know, to heal all of us unproductive sinners, to make our lives productive and fit for service in the kingdom of God! Oh, and I almost forgot, thanks, Jeff, for that inspiring sermon!

Your friend in Christ,
George Denn

December 31, 2000

A s I sit here this New Year's Eve thinking about the holidays, I just can't help thanking God for my many blessings this past year. I remember a year ago today Terry, Tim, and I were coming home from fishing at Lake of the Woods and the hot topic of the day was what was going to happen at midnight Y2K. What happened? Absolutely nothing! This year the Denn clan celebrated Thanksgiving at my sister Jane's home in rural Waterville, not very far as the crow flies from the famous Morris Estate. My sister opened with prayer, and we went around the room telling about something we were thankful for. After a few tearjerkers and hearty laughs, we had another great family Thanksgiving. I couldn't help reminding my sister about the Thanksgiving when she opened the oven door real quick and at the same time she was putting her head down to look in the oven, the oven ignited and a flame shot out and singed her hair. What a gas! Perhaps that is why our family's motto is "Never a Dull Moment"! In the evening I went to Tony Foty's house. Everyone had a kernel of corn in remembrance of what the Pilgrims had to eat at the first Thanksgiving. One by one each person dropped his or her kernel of corn in the jar and told something they were thankful for. I said I was thankful I wasn't a Pilgrim because corn that way isn't very good. Believe me, I know, I used to eat it (unbeknownst to my mother). Growing up on a farm you just sort of do things like that!

Christmas is a time of year we Christians celebrate the birth of Christ, and I love the holiday, just as I love my Lord and savior Jesus Christ! Christmas Eve was celebrated at Mom and Dad's. My nephews gave me 108 cans of Pepsi and a box full of candy; so much for my ever-increasing waistline! I can't help but think of the many Christmases spent here on the farm, and I get awful misty-eyed and happy all at once. I just thank God for the parents I have and the way they raised us. I wouldn't trade them for every single dollar in the world. Thanks Mom and Dad! Christmas Day I went to Waseca again for breakfast with Joe and Delores Osborne, friends of mine from Eagle Lake Church of Christ. That is the great thing about knowing a lot of people — there's always somewhere to go! Dinner was at my Uncle Lowell's in Waseca, and I got to talk with aunts, uncles, and cousins, and then for supper I went to Tony Foty's again. It was a blessed Christmas.

Although I catch myself looking back at special times we have had in the past, I can't help but think of the future. How will it be? What will I be doing? One thing I do know is that I want to be doing God's will, and I look forward to the day when Jesus returns as King of kings and Lord of lords, and I tell you my friends, that day will really be something!

Your brother in Christ,
George Denn

January 15, 2001

—∞∞∞—

Lately my sister Jane has been going through things in the upstairs of my old farmhouse. Most of these things belonged to my mother. She was saving all these things because she thought she might use them some day, but now it is all useless stuff because of decay and being outdated, so we all have the fun job of throwing these things away.It has been reminding me a lot of **Matthew 6:19-21**: *Do not store up for yourselves treasures on earth, where moth and rust destroy, and where thieves break in and steal. But store up for yourselves treasures in heaven, where moth and rust do not destroy, and where thieves do not break in and steal. For where your treasure is, there your heart will be also.*My sister found a writing of mine up there that I had completely forgotten about. I wrote it the night before my grandpa's funeral back in November of 1994 in my pre-Christian days. I thought I would share it with you all here in its original version.

Memories of my Grandpa Aloysius Paul Denn

Last night I couldn't sleep so I wrote this for my remembrance of Grandpa. As I am sure we all have our own favorite memories, I let my mind travel back through the years to my childhood days. I remember Grandpa by the bib overalls that he wore, "Big Macs" and OshKosh. He wore mostly seed corn hats tilted slightly to one side of his head. He liked Right Cut chewing tobacco that he kept in his overall pocket,or in a drawer in the kitchen, the far one on the left, and in the glove box in the car. He also liked North Star beer that was in a case in the porch by the freezer, and maybe something stronger in a hiding place outside that Grandma wouldn't know about. Grandpa also liked popcorn, which was made any time day or night. I remember Grandpa frying hamburgers and boiling potatoes at noon.

Grandpa always took a short break after dinner to rest and watch "As the World Turns"! Grandpa always got up early! — 4:00 to 4:30 to milk cows. I suspect now that Grandpa was sometimes nervous. He was always on the go, and if something bothered him, or if he was sick, he would never say anything about that. Grandpa let me drive his tractors when we were out of Grandma's sight because she would disapprove if she knew I was driving them. Grandpa liked to drive fast, and I do mean FAST!!! I remember Grandma saying on many occasions, "Allie, slow down!!!"

As I grew into my teens and my early twenties, I was fortunate to be able to work side by side with Grandpa, mostly in hayfields and around livestock, cutting wood and in the soybean fields.Grandpa's favorite sayings were" It'sacorker"or"That's a fright!"… or something a little stronger if something really went wrong.

Grandpa wasn't rich by any means, and he wasn't a perfect father. But, he did show love and kindness to his family, and they loved and respected him. At least I did, and for that reason I will always remember Grandpa being a very successful man!

If I had to write that today I wouldn't change a single word. I will add this though:Grandpa always went to church. Idon't recall himever missing a Sunday, and it was through my Grandpa's church's teaching that I knew there was a God and Jesus Christ to cry out to when my ways wouldn't work anymore. I have come to realize in my life, and from all that is written above, that unless you're living your life for Jesus Christ and your work is for Jesus Christ, all that you do is for nothing!

Your friend in Christ,
George Denn

March 25, 2001

———⊱⊰———

L ast Saturday afternoon I had about 1 1/2 hours before Bible
study and church, and I thought I would sneak across a neigh
bor's field and retrieve some round bales of hay that were in a low
piece of ground that I had procrastinated about picking up last fall! I
had started picking them up two days earlier, but I had some trouble
with the new tractor that I felt the Lord blessed me with. It is kind
of ironic. The reason I bought this tractor was so I wouldn't have
breakdowns like I did with the old one. My neighbor and landlord
Daryl has a machine shop, and thankfully he came to my rescue and
fixed a hydraulic line and got me going again.

I am really writing this story in tribute to all of my good neighbors who are always there for me when I am in a pinch; and believe
me, I feel they've helped me in far more ways than I have ever
helped them.

There are three scriptures that I am always reminded of when I
think of my good neighbors:

James 2:8: *If you really keep the royal law found in Scripture,
"Love your neighbor as yourself," you are doing right.*

Leviticus 19:18: *Do not seek revenge or bear a grudge
against one of your people, but love your neighbor as your
self. I am the LORD.*

Matthew 22:37-39: *Jesus replied: "Love the Lord your God
with all your heart and with all your soul and with all your*

*mind." This is the first and greatest commandment. And the
second is like it: Love your neighbor as yourself.*

Anyway, back to the story. I was driving my tractor across snow
banks and through mud. This tractor is a big, orange four-wheel-
drive, and it kind of looks like a big pumpkin so I call it the Great
Pumpkin. I'm thinking as I drive along, *Man, this thing can go
through anything*; it sure is a long way from the old WC you had to
start with a crank that I drove as a youth on my dad's farm. For those
of you who cannot relate to tractors, it is like the difference between
a Model T Ford and today's Lincoln! I was picking up the last bale
when my tractor broke through the ice and was stuck. I had to walk
about a quarter of a mile through knee deep slush and snow which,
by the way, was filling up my boots and freezing my feet as I went.
This time my neighbor Terry from across the road was there when
I needed him, and I asked if he could help me get my tractor pulled
out. He immediately stopped what he was doing. He had 60 feet
of chain and his big 300-plus horsepower 4-wheeldrive tractor, and
we went over to where my tractor was stuck, but all we managed to
do was break several chains. We had to go get more log chains and
shovels. I needed dry clothes. I was feeling kind of down about this
and was wondering if we were going to get it out. I was messing up
my neighbor's day and missing Bible study. Terry said, "George,
one way or another we will get it out." I decided to go home and put
on some dry clothing. Before I went back over I stopped and said
a short prayer. I humbly asked God to help us get the tractor out. I
drove back to Terry's house. We drove his tractor across the field,
shoveled snow from under the stuck tractor, and hooked up 80 feet
of log chain with two semi tires in between for cushion. Out pops
my tractor! The first thing I said was "Praise the Lord!!" I was and
always will be very appreciative of my neighbors. Terry said that
wasn't quite how he imagined his afternoon would be! I said my
days weren't always disasters and thanked him for his help. I even
made church that day by the width of a gnat's eyelash.

Thanks again to my neighbors Daryl and Terry, as well as all my
many other neighbors who have helped me over the years when I've
been in need.

Jesus Christ is like the good neighbor, and this Easter season let us call to mind what Jesus did for mankind at the cross. He was beaten, whipped, spat on, harassed, had spikes driven through his hands and feet, and was left hanging on a cross to die for the sins of all mankind. But no matter what - Jesus was going to do whatever it took to save us from eternal death in hell. For those who haven't accepted Him as their savior yet, He still will do whatever it takes to save you from eternal death. All you have to do is ASK HIM.

Your friend in Christ,
George Denn

May 10, 2001

—∞—

As I write this entry, I am staying at the Double Tree Hotel in a suburb of St. Louis, Missouri, on the seventh floor in Room 722! Some of my good friends back home are probably wondering, "What is George doing in Missouri when he should be home planting corn?" The simple answer is that I'm taking care of the important things first! When Jesus says in Matthew 4:19 to "come follow me and I will make you fishers of men," immediately in verse 20 we are told that "at once they left their nets and followed him." Notice what it doesn't say — it doesn't say they followed him only after they'd first gotten done with what they were doing! Following Jesus can get pretty exciting at times! Right now I am at the District Leadership Conference of the Worldwide Church of God for my district. So far the topics that have been discussed are church finances and making disciples, which is something that is mighty important to whatever church you may belong. Saturday's topics were stewardship with the Gospel and our money, and there was a talk from our Pastor General on the commission of the church, and then we had break-out sessions. The two sessions I attended were youth ministry discussion and principles of conflict resolution. On Sunday morning we had a talk on racial reconciliation, and then we finished the conference with an offering and a communion service. I can't help but look back at the week I endured before I came to this conference. I was back home in Minnesota planting oats. I wanted to get my corn planted before I left, but I couldn't because of rain! Tuesday while I was working up a field for oats, Mike Berg, a young fellow who used to work for me, stopped by. I had the opportunity to share the Gospel of Jesus Christ with him, and then I gave him a Bible and invited him to church. What an exciting day. The rain held off that day so I could finish planting oats. I found out later that only two miles south of where I'd been planting that day there had been a half-inch of rain. Does God take care of us, or what?

Thursday was wild getting ready for this trip and tying up loose ends at home. Thanks to my friend Tony for the check for $215 that he gave me for some corn he bought from me! It will make him feel better knowing I used it for the Lord's work on this trip. My friend Tim picked me up at 3pm Thursday afternoon. We drove till 6pm and ate at Happy Chef in Story City, Iowa, approximately 35 miles west of Liscomb, Iowa, a little town I discovered a year ago in April. (Hello to all the great folks in Liscomb!) . Especially Pete and Linda Peterson, the minister and his wife from the Church of Christ in Liscomb. We spent the night north of Kansas City, and then continued on in the morning. It took us about ten hours to get to the conference. We would have gotten there sooner but we stopped to eat several times!

As I leave this conference, I'm in a better frame of mind then when I came. I remember the inspiring music and messages and as we travel back over the roads heading home. I want to finish this writing by just saying this: For those of you who have answered the call of Jesus Christ, you know how exciting that can be! For those who haven't, I encourage you to do so, for if you answer the call of Jesus Christ, He will take you down many roads that you hardly would have dreamed possible!

Your friend in Christ,
George Denn

June 1, 2001

———— ∞∞∞ ————

I had my day pretty much planned out for today. The first thing I did was to return some hayracks to Jerome and Julie Sieberg, who are long-time friends of mine and also fellow Christians. Then I ran around getting a few parts for a baler — so much for my idea of new equipment not having any problems! I arrived home about 10:30 am and was going to fix the baler and finish baling the load of hay that I didn't get done the evening before, but God has His plans and I have mine, and if my plans aren't the same as His, then guess whose plans get to change?! You guessed it — MINE! Can anyone out there relate to that? My friend, Tony Foty, stopped by and said, "We should get something to eat." It looked like it might rain, and for those who don't understand, rain and hay just don't mix very well, but I thought it probably wouldn't rain until later and I'd get the hay baled just fine. Besides, they had predicted rain for two days and it hadn't rained yet. So Tony said, "Where should we go?" I said, "Old Country Buffet." On the way I told Tony that I had seen Jerome and Julie earlier that morning and when we got inside to eat, and there was Jerome and Julie! And Julie said, "It's a funny thing, Jerome and I were just talking about you, George, on our way here." What are the chances of that happening? Now there is nothing better then getting to talk with other Christians, but today was especially interesting; Jerome and Julie are members of the Catholic Church, Tony Foty is a member of the Evangelical Free Church, and I am a member of the Worldwide Church of God, and then here comes some members of the Church of Christ, Bob Scribner and his wife, Marion. I introduced them to all my friends at the table. About that time I started thinking about Ephesians 4:1-16 — unity in the body of Christ! Though we all have our separate views on biblical things, one common bond we have is that Jesus Christ is our Lord and Savior. Someday in eternal life there won't be all these different denominations and churches, just Christians, but why do we have to wait till eternity to get along? Why not accept one another now? Romans 14 also talks about this. While we're having this great conversation I notice it is raining, so now I can enjoy our conversation longer without thinking of work. I also can't help but remember Matthew 5:45 where it says that God sends rain on the righteous and the unrighteous. Some days I feel like I fit into the wrong category, but God's Word is true, so I know that I am in the right category.

After lunch I spent the rest of my day doing things that I hadn't planned on getting done, and as I write this entry and think back over my day, I can't help but think how perfect my day was. Thanks, God, for changing my plans!

Your friend in Christ,
George Denn

July 20, 2001

---·⊶⊷·---

I just returned home from a fishing weekend in northern Minnesota, and the first message on my answering machine was from my neighbor, Bob, saying, "George, Harvey died." I was halfway expecting a call like that because Harvey wasn't doing too well before I left.

Harvey was a neighbor of my parents and myself for over thirty years. His place is always the first thing I see as I come down my driveway about a mile across the field. Harvey hasn't lived there for a few years, but I'll always think of it as Harvey's Place. They asked me if I would be one of the pallbearers and I gladly accepted.

I sort of sighed when I heard this sad message. It seemed like I'd had a hectic week already, and I wasn't feeling too well to boot, but this sort of thing is more important anyway. Death tends to refocus us on the important things in life. Harvey was a bus driver and a farmer for most of the time I knew him. I remember when I started kindergarten I was really scared, so Harvey kindly took me to my classroom. It was little things like that that I remember about Harvey. Also, back before we had many farm chemicals, the weeds on Harvey's farm were very plentiful and you could always see Harvey out hoeing weeds, which was a common practice in that day. Harvey's wife had a mental illness that he had to deal with. I cultivated Harvey's corn one year when he was having problems getting his crop in. It felt good to be able to help him out. Of all the people I know, I think Harvey had the toughest go of it here on earth. A few years back Harvey told me he was getting married and moving to town. I remember telling him that I thought that was all right!

As I sat and listened to the minister give Harvey's eulogy, I was astounded at the influence Harvey had on people's lives. The minister calculated that Harvey influenced 210,000 kids in the years he drove the school bus. I know I was one of those 210,000, but I bet this number would be greater if someone added up all the people he came in contact with in his entire life. Harvey was a simple man, but this man had a great influence on my life and now he had gone on to receive his heavenly reward.

Jesus Christ is the ultimate example we humans have. His name is also the only name under heaven through which we can be saved (Acts 4:12). I sometimes wonder in my own life, *am I influencing people in the way God intended or am I living for myself?* Everyperson we come in contact with — even if it is for a second or for a lifetime — we have influenced for either good or bad. God helps us all to be the people He wants us to be.

Your friend in Christ,
George Denn

August 5, 2001

It is small-grain harvest time on my farm, and as I ride the swather back and forth across the fields of tall rye, pillowy wheat, and grainy oats, I hear the snitch, snitch, snitch of the sickle cutting the grain while watching the reel turning and laying the cut grain on the canvas, which then deposits the grain in the center of the machine and forms a windrow ready for the combine. It is hot, it is humid, and the engine is behind me — (in my words) "Hotter than the lid on a kitchen stove!" I have noticed something interesting while I am cutting: weeds and grain are cut together and deposited in the windrow. I considered the parable of the wheat and weeds, as told in Matthew 13: 24-30. I have sown the grain, but the weeds come up naturally. As the combine makes its way through the fields gobbling up the windrows, the grain is thrashed from the stalk inside this great machine and goes through the separating process and is then deposited in the tank for loading on trucks to be hauled to town or put in a bin. The straw, chaff, light kernels, and weeds all get thrown out the back of the machine and tossed on the ground, useless for anything but animal bedding; it will eventually be spread back on the land in the form of manure. My thoughts at this time run to Revelation 14:14-20, where we are told of the harvesting of souls on the earth ... just as the oats, wheat, and rye have different purposes, so do we as human beings on this earth, and if we are God's people we need to take this calling we have dead serious. Just as it is with a grain crop, there is only a certain amount of time to do this harvest. Harvest too early and all you have is a pile of moldy grain. Harvest too late and you have a lot of grain that is shelling, which is caused by storms and wind. The crop may become lodged, making the harvest slow and difficult. It is my prayer that we have our eyes opened by God and get busy with the harvest. Jesus tells us to ask Him to send workers into His harvest fields (Matthew 9:37). It's time to open our eyes, folks; we are either the weeds or the wheat, and we need to act like the one we are. Hopefully I am not writing to any weeds. I will leave you with Jesus' own words in *John 4:35: "Do you not say, 'Four months more and then the harvest?' I tell you,* **open your eyes and look** *at the fields! They are ripe for harvest."*

Your friend in Christ,
George Denn

September 3, 2001

—∞∞∞—

As I write this story I'm sitting outside my house on September 2 at 11 pm, and the scene before me just captivates me so much that I just have to take a pen and write. The bright full moon is high in the sky lighting my cornfield that I have half cut, with corn shocks standing in the moonlight that is also dancing on the lake east of the cornfield. The light filtering out from my kitchen window provides just enough visibility for me to write this. Once again I see standing corn and corn shocks and smell the aroma of cut corn, and my thoughts run to Genesis 1:1: In the beginning God created the heavens and the earth. As we read on in Genesis, by the time He'd finished creating us humans, on the sixth day He said "it is very good" concerning all that He had created. And all of it was very good, but then sin entered into the world, and in my words that was very bad.

Human beings have been disconnected from their maker ever since. That is what sin does to us – it separates us from God — but God also provided a way for us humans to get back into a right relationship with Him, and that was the sacrifice of His very own son Jesus Christ. Jesus Himself says in **John 14:6**, *"I am the way and the truth and the life. No one comes to the Father except through me."* Jesus was willing to die for you, for me, and for everyone in the whole world. As a matter of fact, the only sin Jesus can't forgive is the sin of walking away from that sacrifice. Jesus can't forgive someone who doesn't want forgiveness. **Romans 6:23:** *"For the wages of sin is death, but the gift of God is eternal life in Christ Jesus our Lord."*

This is very good news for everyone; let me use an analogy from my pumpkin patch to show how this good news spreads. I saved two pumpkins for seed last year; one had 500 seeds and one had 800 seeds, which is a total of 1,300 seeds, or about a thousand growing plants. Those plants will produce about three to six pumpkins each so that is roughly 4,500 pumpkins from the original two pumpkins used for seed. With an average market value of $2 each, that is $9,000 earned from the original two pumpkins. Just as pumpkin vines spread across the field covering everything, so eventually will the gospel of Jesus Christ cover the world. So don't think your Christian witness isn't important; just remember the two pumpkins. They only had a market value of $2 each.

Your friend in Christ,
George Denn

October 29, 2001

Luke 11:4: *Forgive us our sins, for we also forgive everyone who sins against us.*

That verse is part of "The Lord's Prayer" or "The Our Father." I prayed that prayer all the years growing up as a Catholic boy until I no longer attended a Catholic church. I said that prayer last year at the prayer service for my grandma's funeral that I officiated. I said that prayer just last week at my neighbor's wake during the prayer service. I have come to realize that saying that prayer is very easy, but living that prayer is quite a lot harder! This year I had three places where I was selling pumpkins, corn shocks, and straw for fall decorations. It is sold on the honor system, and I thought I would help my church, the Worldwide Church of God, by tithing 10 percent of the proceeds and donating 50 percent of the sales from one location to my good friends at Church of Christ in Eagle Lake for their new church building fund. The first couple of weeks went fine with Pastor Jeff taking care of the Eagle Lake location. Then one night I went to check the box and noticed the lock was missing, and the first thing I thought was *I think I have been robbed! Open the lid ... I know that I have been robbed because there is no money where money is supposed to be!* That taught me a lesson that I need to get the money before dark. Then I started getting phone calls from friends telling me things like, "George, there is no lock on your box at Elysian," and, "We found a cut lock on the Eagle Lake box," all in broad daylight. This went on for a good two weeks almost every day, or so it seems as I remember it, all good weather days during the busy harvest, but I am unable to get much done because of these crooks. One day the whole box was torn off at the Elysian location, so we did a stake-out with no luck. The two churches were praying for these thieves to be caught; besides robbing me, they were robbing from God, and He probably didn't like that very much either. I started to lose my patience with whoever this was. I had spent $145 on new locks, two new boxes, and diversions in the lids. Later on I made the comment that if I had to watch for these guys myself, I was probably going to open the back of someone's pants with my double-barrel 12-gauge shotgun, but I had to get a hold of myself because THAT IS NOT WHAT JESUS WOULD DO!

Everything just fell into place on Monday the 22nd of October. When the thieves were trying to rob the Elysian location, my brother-in-law just happened to be driving by, and he got close enough in a high-speed chase to get the license number of the vehicle. How's that for a Baptist brother Thanks, Tim, I owe you one. I called the sheriff in that county and they couldn't trace the plates. When I just happened to stop for coffee in Madison Lake, the storeowner said that from the description of the car it sounded like someone he knew from an episode that occurred in his store. I got home and called my friend Jeff to tell him about this, and he said, "Guess what – we've been robbed at the Eagle Lake location." I called the Blue Earth County Sheriff and gave him all the information from the license plate and car description, and in two hours he had all the robbers apprehended, with full confessions from the five that were involved, ages 15 to 19 years.

The very next day I got a phone call from one of these young fellows who said that he wanted to apologize. I said I would like to see him in person, so he and his sister came out and we had a long talk. I got the opportunity to share the Gospel of Jesus Christ with these two, and they said they would come to church Saturday evening, but they didn't come and I was disappointed in that. Two others came later in the day with their parents and I had an interesting talk with them also. I hope now that four out of the five are on the road to being responsible people, because as I look back on my own life, I can see some things I did that, if I would have continued, would have led to the same consequences.

I want all of you out there to do me a favor; stop and say a prayer for these five young people, that the Lord would touch their lives. Yes, I have forgiven these five, including the one I have never seen or heard from (I guess I have to leave him to God). I can see how the Lord has made great progress in my life, but praying *forgive us our trespasses as we forgive those who trespass against us* is far harder than just saying those words. It takes God's hand to change a person's heart so they can pray that sincerely, and no matter how hard it is to let God do that in your life, the rewards are far greater than any pain it takes in getting there.

Your friend in Christ,
George Denn

December 3, 2001

~∞∞~

A s I write this entry I am reminded of **Ecclesiastes 3:1:** *There is a time for everything and a season for every activity under heaven.* For the second time on November 11th I've had a semi truck in my yard. Seven years ago to the day I sold the milk cows. This time my beef stock cows went to town. On hand to help were my Dad, Chris, and Jeremy Schenk, the young fellows with the truck. The first time I met them was in 1981 when Jeremy was about four years old. Now Chris and Jeremy drive semi trucks and I write these inspired articles! How times have changed! Anyway, for the last 39 years of my life, cows have been a daily part of my life, either directly or indirectly. Now that I've sold the cows, my hired man, Troy, is ripping up all the fences, so if I want cows again I will have to put up all that fencing again. But in this stage of my life, believe me, it is not going to happen! I always enjoyed the cows, especially watching them go into the pasture on the first day in the springtime when the mother cows are attending to their newborn calves. There is also a down side to tending cattle, though, and my hat's off to anyone God gives the calling to do so, because I know the drudgery of what men have to go through to take care of cattle — frozen hands and feet, getting kicked, watching one die when you did your best to keep it alive. I believe the Lord's calling me to other things. At this time I don't know what it is, but I'll know when I get there because God will show me. Seven years ago I was sad to see the cows go and I was worried about what I was going to do. But I've seen all the things Jesus has worked out in my life, and I am really excited about the future. Selling those cows was something the Lord had been impressing upon me for quite awhile, so I feel good that I obeyed him.

I'm reminded of **Hosea 10:12:** *Sow for yourselves righteousness, reap the fruit of unfailing love, and break up your unplowed ground; for it is time to seek the Lord until he comes and showers righteousness upon you.*

So as my life goes on until its final destination when the Lord calls me home, I will continually give up things that the Lord asks of me. I will trust more and more in the living Christ as He leads me in this present life. I ask all of you who read these words to say a prayer for me, and I just want to say a short prayer for all of you, that we will have the ears to hear and the eyes to see what the Lord is telling us this day. I'll close with Jesus' own words **Revelations 2:7, 11, 17, 29; 3:6, 13, 22:** *"He who has an ear let him hear what the Spirit says to the churches."*

Your friend in Christ,
George Denn

December 28, 2001

I was looking out of the kitchen window thinking of something to do. I thought I would wander out into the woods and burn a brush pile that has been building up for the past five years. On my way I decided I would burn a great big basswood tree that was pretty much dead except for one or two branches. It was completely hollow and I could stand up inside it. This once massive, beautiful tree was now a dead hulk, pretty much useless anymore, and being basswood it would not make good firewood. Also, it stood by the old pasture gate next to the field, so it would not damage the crops if I burned it now. A little diesel fuel and a couple of matches and I created a fire in the hollow trunk of the tree.

I walked over to the brush pile, which also contained our old church piano and table, Terry's old chair, scraps from Graham's house and other things contributed from various people I've known over the last five years.

While I was lighting the brush pile, I was thinking of **John 15:5-6**. Jesus said, *"I am the vine; you are the branches. if a man remains in me and I in him, he will bear much fruit; apart from me you can do nothing. If anyone does not remain in me, he is like a branch that is thrown away and withers; such branches are picked up, thrown into the fire and burned."*

I was thinking about how there are tons of people who don't know the Lord on a personal level, and those of us who do know Him but don't share our faith in Jesus Christ when the opportunity arises are like these dead branches on my brush pile. About that time Mitch, my nephew, and his friend drive up teasing me that I am smoking out the squirrels in a hollow tree, but then they went fishing on a lake that has no fish, so I am wondering who is the silly one here!

I walked back to the burning tree, and as I see flames and smoke belching out of hollow places in the tree, I start wondering how old that tree was — maybe 150, 200 years old, but today is the end of the road for this big fellow, and all my years here I have marveled at its size. When my nephews were small I called it the Keebler tree! What it was like here when this tree started growing only God knows.

As the huge limbs started falling and then finally as the big trunk toppled into the fire, I considered how man is somewhat like this tree. Planted in God's creation, we grow up and become useful, and then we grow old until one day we are eliminated from the face of this earth in the form of death, and all we that we have done will be consumed, just like the fire consumed the tree.

Thankfully for us human beings there is a Savior, Jesus Christ, God's one and only Son who suffered the usual and grisly form of Roman execution, with spikes driven through His hands and feet as He was nailed to the cross for my sins and yours; he was buried and then rose from the dead on the third day, and He is seated at the right hand of God the Father (Hebrews 1:3). And now we have the opportunity of everlasting life.

> **John 3:35–36:** *The Father loves the Son and has placed everything in his hands. Whoever believes in the Son has eternal life, but whoever rejects the Son will not see life, for God's wrath remains on him.*

So how do you want to spend eternity?
Your friend in Christ,
George Denn

February 2, 2002

L ately I have been learning how to run a new machine. It is called "a computer!" Probably most of you have one, but I know a few of you don't, and I have resisted buying one until now. It reminds me of what Jesus told Peter in John 21:18: *"Feed my sheep. I tell you the truth, when you were younger you dressed yourself and went where you wanted; but when you are old you will stretch out your hands, and someone else will dress you and lead you where you do not want to go."*

Personally, I was determined to never own one of these contraptions. I always thought they were stupid. Besides, I am more at home riding a tractor, chasing a cow, or sitting on a stump out in the woods watching animals, or lying quietly up in the haymow watching door-to-door salespeople and an occasional minister thinking they were going to catch me at home. Now that is what I call fun! But times change and it looks like computers are here to stay, and I've known enough people in my lifetime who resisted changes that we now consider basic living, such as the telephone, electricity, and indoor toilets. I knew I didn't want to end up like the people I could remember who had resisted these things. As I recall, these folks lived with a disadvantage compared to people who had such amenities. It always takes me forever to change, but once I finally do I always wonder why I didn't change sooner.

This reminds me of my Christian conversion. Before I became a Christian, I had always thought people who ran around calling Jesus their Lord and Savior were nuts. I went to church on occasion and figured I was a good enough Christian; besides, I had other plans. But I've come to find out that if your plans and the Lord's plans are not the same, someone gets to change their plans, and believe me, it isn't the Lord who changes His! After much pain and anguish I came to recognize Jesus as my Lord and Savior and that these Christians weren't nuts after all, and now I have something I didn't have before, which is eternal life.

John 6:40: *"For my Father's will is that everyone who looks to the Son and believes in him shall have eternal life, and I will raise him up at the last day."*

I don't know about you, but to me it is very comforting to know that! As a matter of fact, the only sin God cannot forgive is if you walk away from the Savior and don't come back. He can hardly forgive someone who absolutely does not want forgiveness.

Matthew 11:12: *From the days of John the Baptist until now, the kingdom of heaven has been forcefully advancing, and forceful men lay hold of it.*

So, just as people who resist change are at a great disadvantage compared to the people around them who have accepted it, so are the people who haven't accepted Jesus Christ as Lord and Savior, except their disadvantage will be spending eternity in HELL literally. Please take some time today to read Revelation 20:11-15 and Revelation 22.

Your friend in Christ,
George Denn

March 2, 2002

⚬⚬⚬

A couple of days ago I received what looked somewhat like a letter in the mail. It was addressed to Hay By George Denn from Mose S. Borntreger. I opened up the letter and saw that it was an Auction Sale Bill. The auction sale was to be held on Mose's farm on March 2.

Mose is Amish, and I met him two years ago about this time of year. The previous fall my corn binder broke down while binding corn for my autumn bundles that I sell with pumpkins. So I had to find parts for the machine somewhere, being this is an antique piece of machinery circa 1920, but at least I had a year to find the parts. About the same time the *AgriNews* paper subscription was due and I almost canceled it. At the last minute I changed my mind and reordered. In February, I noticed an Amish auction advertised in that paper. *Ah ha, corn binder parts!* I thought. I have read many books on the Amish people but have never met any firsthand, so I made my way about ten miles southwest of Leroy, Minnesota, to the sale and I did buy a binder for parts. A week later I went back with my neighbor George to pick up my binder and got the opportunity to meet Mose and his brother. We helped them fix a wagon wheel axle that they had bent that day hauling logs. I went to another auction sale in the area about six weeks later and ran into Mose again. I found a raccoon in a threshing machine that day and it caused such a commotion that they stopped the auction for a bit.

I learned Amish people are a little hard to get acquainted with, so I was surprised to hear from him again. I saw Mose at the sale today and I asked if he remembered me? He said, "Hay by George." I told

Mose I got a sale bill from him, and he said he'd mailed it thinking that it might get me down here again. After I left Mose to get a cup of coffee, here comes Larry Attenberger and Marv Gartner, two people that I have known for many years from Mapleton, Minnesota. I think they were about as surprised to see me as I was to see them, considering we were 130 miles from home. I stayed until 2 o'clock, but decided to leave as I was getting cold and also because I wanted to make it to our CARE meeting at church. As I drove home I was thinking this story might make a good entry for this book. I consider Mose and myself as men who are each following the same God in our own way; we each have the same Jesus Christ for the atonement for our sins and are led by the same Holy Spirit. Yet we are vastly different. I have great respect for the Amish people; in some ways they are way ahead of their Christian counterparts, and I wouldn't ever want them to change the way they live and do things, for they are a very unique people (and I am sure misunderstood by some).

> **Romans 14:7-12:** *For none of us lives to himself alone and none of us dies to himself alone. If we live we, live to the Lord; and if we die, we die to the Lord. So, whether we live or die, we belong to the Lord. For this very reason, Christ died and returned to life so that he might be the Lord of both the dead and the living. You, then, why do you judge your brother? Or why do you look down on your brother? For we will all stand before God's Judgment seat. It is written: "As surely as I live," says the Lord, "every knee will bow before me; every tongue will confess to God." so then, each of us will give an account of himself to God.*

Thanks, Mose, for inviting me to the sale. Hope to see you again sometime!

Your friend in Christ,
George Denn

May 26, 2002

———— ⌇ ————

John 12:24-26: *I tell you the truth, unless a kernel of wheat falls to the ground and dies, it remains only a single seed. But if it dies, it produces many seeds. The man who loves his life will lose it, while the man who hates his life in this world will keep it for eternal life. Whoever serves me must follow me; and where I am, my servant also will be. My Father will honor the one who serves me.*

I was cleaning up the scrap metal on my place the other day and I decided it was high time that the one piece that had survived the scrap metal drives here in the past was going this time! This piece of iron sat there in the same place like an icon for forty years with gooseberry bushes growing up around it. My woods will never be the same now that it is gone. This piece of machinery was a Minnesota hay loader made by the prisoners in Stillwater State Prison in Minnesota probably 60 to 80 years ago. My dad bought it for only $5.00 from the owner of a farm that he lived on at one time. That was when Dad was twenty-seven years old, and now he is seventy. This was a great invention for its day because it could do as much work as it would've taken five men using pitchforks, but then once hay balers came on the scene, it was made obsolete almost immediately. It was already in the obsolete category when Dad purchased it! But he used it for three years, and then a tree fell on it and broke a few of the loading boards. So he pulled it into the woods, and there it sat for forty years doing nothing. I bet I can put up more hay in twenty minutes with my round baler than two men could put up all day with a hay loader!

I almost stopped myself a couple times from getting rid of it, but finally I loaded it up and, like a sacrifice bound to an altar, I log-chained it down high up on my truck so the wind wouldn't blow it off and onto the roadway, and then off I went to the scrap yard. A great big claw-like crane picked up Dad's hay loader and dumped it in a crusher. After that it was loaded on a railroad car and hauled to a smelter to be used again. Maybe that new car that some wealthy person bought was really my dad's old hay loader, or maybe it became some modern piece of farm machinery or just about anything made of steel.

God has a purpose for mankind, a physical purpose on this earth — the message of reconciliation as he talks about in 2 Corinthians 5:11-6:2. His purpose is to save us from the evil power that is on the earth (Ephesians 2:1-3). Jesus Christ, God's very own Son was sent into the world to redeem mankind, and those who understand and believe must all be conformed to God's Word. Some may think this is all foolishness, but only those who are perishing.

1 Corinthians 1:18: *For the message of the cross is foolishness to those who are perishing, but to us who are being saved it is the power of God.*

Your friend in Christ,
George Denn

November 30, 2002

⎯⎯⎯⎯⎯⎯

Psalm 100:3-5: *Know that the Lord is God. It is he who made us, and we are his; we are his people, the sheep of his pasture. Enter his gates with thanksgiving and his courts with praise; give thanks to him and praise his name. For the Lord is good and his love endures forever; his faithfulness continues through all generations.*

As I sit here early this Thanksgiving morning listening to the wood fire crackling in the stove, the first thing I am thankful for is a warm house. My church will prepare a meal for homeless people on Sunday, and some of these people live under a bridge in Mankato.This whole week has caused me to consider what God has done for me this past year and throughout my entire life. I was cutting a tree the other day for to make logs for some new hayracks. My friend Jeff counted its rings, and together we determined it was over 135 years old. I stopped to consider how God knew 135 years ago what that tree would be used for and who would use it. Now the wood is a blessing to me and to everyone else who I gave some of the wood to.My chain saw broke on Tuesday, which turned into a blessing because if it hadn't been broken I probably would've been working yesterday at cutting more wood, and I would've missed going on a nice, long walk where I was inspired to write this story. Yesterday was a beautiful late fall day just perfect for a walk. I was looking for something to do so I thought I would take a hike. I walked down past the barn and across a small field to the public landing on the lake. The lake is beautiful; it just froze over three days ago and has about two inches of ice that cracks if you walk on it. Over an old pasture gate and into my neighbor's pasture, I recall walking through here almost daily thirty years ago to play with the neighbors, but now I noticed that the old cow paths that we used to follow are grown up with brush. The big hill we used to slide down is grown up with brush also; I guess those old cows were good for something after all. As I walked along a manmade road, I noticed a big oak tree on a steep hillside standing perfectly straight, its roots embedded deeply into the ground. That tree reminded me of how it is when everything gets taken out from under you and it's only your deep faith in Jesus Christ that holds you up. I also considered all the help that I had needed this year and all the people who had come to my rescue, and I also considered those who were against me in certain things, and I prayed for them because the things of this world have them captured (1 John 2:15-17).

Many thanks to all those who helped me in my times of need; I am also thankful for the lady in the church who said she missed the articles I had written for the church newsletter; that encouraged me to write this one with God's inspiration. As I turned up a hill and walked through another open gate, I noticed this gate has been left opened for quite some time because trees had grown up in between the wires. As I stood in the gateway, I could see my home below from this distance! It's pretty modest by today's standard, but it has character: the view of my farm shows an old, white farmhouse with smoke curling from the chimney, with a red barn and a field in the distance with thirteen shocks of corn standing in it just like a painted autumn scene; I have a passing thought of how badly everything needs paint, but the whole scene just touches my heart.

I am thankful God has placed me here for reasons that I am not completely sure of. I stood there for a while looking at my farm and counting my blessings, and then I hiked back home. As I walked into the house I noticed my old Bible laying there, so I picked it up and read Psalm 139 ... and I found out that God had been with me all along, and for this I am truly thankful!

Your friend in Christ,
George Denn

January 30, 2003

——— ∞∞∞ ———

It always amazes me where ideas for a story come from. Most of the time I wonder if God will ever give me another story to write about. Just when I figure that I might never be inspired again, BAM, He gives me something!

Generally things are pretty boring around here in the winter, so when I get a chance to go somewhere I jump at it. Yesterday at 4 am, Jeff and Peggy Peterson and Dick Pringle and I were on our way to Hubert Humphrey Airport in Minneapolis, Minnesota. Jeff and Peggy had won a short trip to Florida, and I rode along with Dick to take them to the airport.

On the way Dick was telling me of his experiences in the U.S. Air Force. One of the stories he told was about the time he flew to Juneau, Alaska, and apparently there had been a great plane crash in this area days earlier. Evidently to get to Juneau you have to fly through the area called the Three Sisters, a series of mountain peaks, and on the day of the crash it had been very foggy, and all the pilot had to go by was the plane's instrument panel. Evidently the pilot was very nervous even though his instrument panel said he was just fine. He was so nervous in fact that he flew to Anchorage instead of Juneau.

As I listened to Dick tell this story, I thought how it sounded so much like Matthew 6:25-34. In this scripture Jesus is telling His followers not to worry about their lives, money, and earthly things. How often are we like that nervous pilot who could only go by his instrument panel, and instead of trusting those instruments he turned to go a familiar route.

Our Bible is like that instrument panel; anyone following Jesus Christ has to go by its teachings. How often do we turn from biblical instruction and go another familiar route the world has to offer?

Let's heed what Jesus says in **Matthew 6:19-24:** *"Do not store up for yourselves treasures on earth, where moth and rust destroy, and where thieves break in and steal. But store up for yourselves treasures in heaven, where moth and rust do not destroy, and where thieves do not break in and steal. For where your treasure is, there your heart will be also.*

"The eye is the lamp of the body. If your eyes are good, your whole body will be full of light. But if your eyes are bad, your whole body will be full of darkness. If then the light within you is darkness, how great is that darkness!

"No one can serve two masters. Either he will hate the one and love the other, or he will be devoted to the one and despise the other. You cannot serve both God and Money."

If we love God and serve Him, we will follow what His word tell us even if that goes against what the world teaches. Therefore our eyes will be good and our whole body full of light. If we serve money our eyes are bad and the light that is within us is darkness, and how great that darkness is. Who is the Lord in your life? Remember — Lord means master — the one that you serve!

Your brother in Christ,
George Denn

February 19, 2003

——◦◦◦◦◦◦——

Psalm 121:1-2: *I lift my eyes to the hills — where does my help come from? My help comes from the Lord, the maker of heaven and earth.*

Sunday afternoon I received a phone call from my best friend Jeff asking if I could get away for a few days. I asked how soon we would be leaving and he replied as soon as possible, adding mysteriously, "I'll explain later." Now I am as flexible as a rag. So at about 4pm we are on our way. Destination? The Smoky Mountains of Tennessee. Reason? To pray! This was a most interesting trip as we discussed many parts of Scripture, and it seems that God had been showing both of us some interesting things in Scripture. It was just interesting to pick each other's thoughts on things. The first stop on our journey was to visit Jeff's Uncle Pete and Aunt Linda in Liscomb, Iowa. Pete is a pastor in this town, and we were able to take in the church's Sunday night service and participate, and also share some of the things that the Lord had been showing us about money, health, and the necessity of God's people to be distinct and not be caught up in the world around them.Pete put us up for the night, and after a good breakfast from Linda and some deep theological discussions, Pete prayed for us for protection and that God would open our hearts and minds to what the Lord had in store for us as His servants because we didn't have a plan for this journey. Also we didn't have much money; Jeff had a credit card for gas only. I had brought along $190 so it was pretty bare bones! We figured the Lord would provide. Our next stop was in Alburnett, Iowa to see

Jeff's cousin Dan. Dan bought us lunch (the Lord provides!), and after another deep theological discussion Dan showed us the church he pastors and the improvements the congregation has made on the building. Before we left Dan prayed for us. Also he seemed to think it quite interesting that we could just take off on a trip like this.

As we headed into Illinois, Jeff's wife, Peggy, called on the cell phone and gave us the phone number of her cousin. We called and asked if they would let us spend the night. Praise the Lord, they said they would be glad to, and Scott and Gina Ruhl were even making homemade pizza for us when we arrived. We weren't there very long before all four of us realized this was a provision from God — a place for food and shelter for Jeff and me and a chance to talk about some things for Scott and Gina. The next morning Scott called their minister, John Robertson from Mount Pulaski, Illinois, to see if he might pray for us. He said he certainly would and was interested in meeting us. Scott took us to meet his pastor and we all sat down in a conference room in the church. We were telling John and the youth minister about our "Prayer Journey" as we had now started to call it. They laid hands on us and prayed, and then off we went.

We traveled through Illinois, Indiana, Kentucky, and southeast Tennessee to the Great Smoky Mountains of Tennessee down to Knoxville and Gatlinburg. As we passed through Gatlinburg it was starting to get dark, and the town was lit up with glitz and glitter, restaurants, shops, dance halls, and theaters, but that wasn't what we came here for.

We had come to meet God on a mountain, so up, up, around, and around as high as the road went, we climbed. We parked the pickup, and then each of us went off to be alone with his Creator. As I looked across the mountains on this starry moonlit night, I thought of Moses and Elijah when they went to meet God on the mountain, and then I thought of Peter, James, and John as they witnessed the transfiguration of Jesus and the voice of God saying, "This is My Son whom I love, with him I am well pleased. Listen to Him!" (Matthew 17)
As I communed with God, the Creator of this mountain range, the starry sky and the shining moon, I considered what a huge God I serve, and the glitz and glitter down below that man had created paled significantly in comparison to this sight that God created, and

all this He gave to us to enjoy free of charge, unlike the manmade sights down below. As I looked at the small headlights of cars here and there coming up and down the mountain side, God was telling me *if man can make you a path up the side of a mountain just think of the paths I can make you in the mountains of your life*! I think I will continue to walk the path that God has set before me no matter the cost, because it is the only path that promises eternal life (John 3:16); all others lead to destruction (John 3:36)!

Your brother in Christ,
George Denn

March 20, 2003

Numbers 21:8: *The Lord said to Moses, "Make a snake and put it up on a pole; anyone who is bitten can look at it and live."*

Now I know starting a story with a verse about snakes may seem rather peculiar, but we will see its relevance in this story. Yesterday I got out of bed at four am and made my way to my parents'home in Waseca, Minnesota. I always enjoy driving roads in the early morning. As I neared Waseca a train engine was coming towards me, with bright lights shining! At first it appeared to be close enough to hit me, but as I got closer to the railroad crossing it was apparent that the train would cross over a different road than the one I was on. As I drove along I considered how that bright light reminded me of what our churches need to be — a beacon light to those who are on the wrong road. As I came into town, the train signals were flashing. I hate waiting for trains so I did what I always do, though I don't recommend this to anyone; but racing trains has always been a thrill of mine. Once again I made it through, and I arrived at mom and dad's house with time to spare to drink some coffee before everyone else showed up.My dad, Aunt Marilyn, my sister Jane, and I were taking Mother to Rochester. She is in a test program for a disease she has called Cortical Basil Ganglionic degeneration.Everyone always asks,"What is the disease your mom has?" Now you know why I never remember what it is! This disease is fatal; eventually Mother will die from it. But through my parents' cooperation with this research program, the medical industry is being helped greatly. This sense of gladly helping others has always have been typical of my parents. It is hard to see your mother barely able to remember two or three spoken words. The doctor asked Mother if she ever had dreams, and she said "yes," and he asked what about, and her reply was that she dreamed of canning tomatoes. My sister said, "That sounds more like a nightmare to me!" But if my mother could get out of that wheelchair and walk around, I know she would enjoy every moment. One thing this disease has done is to force Mother and Father to get closer to God and to accept Jesus Christ as their Lord and Savior. Before this mother was a rough-hewn character, and the Lord was not on her mind as He is now. Mother has no earthly cares of money and health, and as I look back over their lives I can see the great hand of God drawing my parents closer to Him and protecting them now in their elder years. Before we all said goodbye and left Mother for the day, we gathered around and prayed for healing for Mother, knowing full well the healing for Mother will probably come when the Lord calls her home, but we asked accordingly to His will and not our own.

So as we read in Numbers 21:8, Moses made a bronze snake and put it on a pole. Then when anyone was bitten by a real snake and then looked at the bronze snake, he lived. This was a foreshadowing of how Jesus would be hung on a cross, bloodied and beaten; but anyone who looks upon Him and sees Him as their Lord and Savior will live eternally with Him.

So we all must look to Jesus Christ for our healing, for our diseases and sickness and for the healing of the breach between humanity and God that's caused by our sins. In other words, no Jesus, no healing, and no eternal life, but ... *know* Jesus, *know* healing, *know* eternal life!

John 3:14: *Just as Moses lifted up the snake in the desert, so the Son of Man must be lifted up, that everyone who believes in Him may have eternal life.*

I don't know about you, but eternal life sounds really great to me, and as far as I know Jesus is the only way there.

Acts 4:12: *Salvation is found in no one else, for there is no other name under heaven given to men by which we must be saved.*

Your brother in Christ,
George Denn

May 18, 2003

—⸎—

Matthew 7:7-8: *Ask and it will be given to you; seek and you will find; knock and the door will be opened to you. For everyone who asks receives; he who seeks finds; and to him who knocks, the door will be opened.*

I was leaving church Saturday after services when my friend Tim said, "George, the church took up a collection for you … here," and he handed me a roll of cash and a couple of checks totaling $2050. I really didn't know quite what to say, so I just took the roll of money and said thanks. I didn't count it until I got home, but before I counted the money I asked God to bless those who gave this a "zillon fold!" I guess this a way to say thank you to all those who helped me this past year and sacrificed greatly to help me out.

Some of you know of my personal financial struggle that started with a feedlot violation more than ten years ago and ended in bank ruptcy last May and the confiscation of all my farm machinery last November. But by the grace of God and a whole lot of help and many things too numerous to mention here, I am still farming today. When I tell people that God must want me to farm, I mean it! If you knew everything that went on at this farm in the last ten years on a daily basis, you would agree there is no logical reason to explain why I should be here right now! I always said you had to be tough to live on this farm, but now I know you need God Almighty watching over you also. You really have to love farming to stay with it, and I know that any man who has tilled the soil and loved doing so knows what I am talking about.

Joel 2:25-26: *I will replay you for the years the locusts have eaten — the great locust and the young locust, the other locusts and the locust swarm — my great army that I sent among you. You will have plenty to eat, until you are full, and you will praise the name of the Lord your God, who has worked wonders for you; never again will my people be shamed.*

I believe that scripture with all my heart. At this time I want to thank each and every one who has helped me, because I have seen the love of Christ in many a man and woman this past year — people with hearts bigger than the haymow door on my barn. God knows who you are and sees the good that you have done. When I compare myself with you all, I feel pale in comparison. Also, thanks to all the members of the Solid Rock Fellowship Church of which I am a member. Words cannot express how touching it is to have people come to help you in your time of need! I want to give back to my church that $2050 over the course of time, because I truly believe that a gift should keep on giving and I hope it can help someone else as much as it has helped me.

Revelation 21:5: *He who was seated on the throne said," I am making everything new!" Then he said, "Write this down, for these words are trustworthy and true."*

I wonder if that is why all this different new equipment is showing up around my place now?! Do you think ...?

Your brother in Christ,
George Denn

July 4, 2003

∞

Matthew 28:18-20: *Then Jesus came to them and said, "All authority in heaven and on earth has been given to me. Therefore go and make disciples of all nations, baptizing them in the name of the Father and of the Son and of the Holy Spirit, and teaching them to obey everything I have commanded you. And surely I am with you always, to the very end of the age."*

As I write this I am sitting on a bench under a huge cottonwood tree on the banks of the Mississippi river about two miles east of my destination, which is a little town called Buffalo, Iowa. It was once the home of a button factory from 1890 to 1910. You can see the shells all along the river where buttons were stamped out, and I brought two shells home for souvenirs.I was hauling hay the other night when my cell phone rang; it was my nephew, Nathan Marcus Denn, and he said, "George, can you come down here and baptize me?" Surprised but happy to hear this sudden announcement, I said, "Sure … when"? He said, "I will let you know tomorrow morning." Nate had been spending a week at the SEP summer camp that my church sponsored. This year camp was at Camp Abe Lincoln two and half miles west of Buffalo, Iowa, which is a six-hour drive from Mankato, Minnesota where I live. Nate is eighteen years old, and we as a church sponsored him. It seemed at one time Nate did not know if he wanted to attend. Nate's interest in the Lord started several years back at another church camp and Bible studies that I used to hold before I spending time baling hay with my nephews. I didn't think at the time that the Bible studies were doing any good, but I guess the seeds that were sown did take root. Galatians 6:9 tells us that at the proper time we will reap a harvest if we do not give up. Speaking of harvest, a grain barge called the Dell Butcher pushes twelve loaded barges down the river; each one holds fifty semi-loads, and it takes thirty days to make the round trip on the river. How is that for patience!

As I drove to the camp I did not realize it then, but I was in for quite an experience. One of the people in charge took me to where Nate was, but I had to wait until they all had returned from an outing. While I was waiting I was able to watch a dance class while they practiced, which was very interesting. When Nate and his group arrived, he introduced me to all his new camp friends. They were from Minnesota, Iowa, Wisconsin, New York, Arkansas, Illinois and many other states, I'm sure, but those are the ones I can remember. The whole camp was full of youthful electricity (this is the only way I can explain the atmosphere), excitement, joy, and camaraderie.

The whole experience just gave me a spiritual lift. I had lunch with everyone, and then afterwards the youth participated in various events such as canoeing, volleyball, archery, soccer, running, and swimming. One thing that I enjoyed observing was the vast difference in personalities among the young people, which is just the way God intended it to be — something that our culture needs to fully comprehend instead of everyone trying to be like someone else.

The most important activity to take place was the baptism ceremonies. Five youths were baptized that day into the fellowship and service of Jesus Christ. The excitement and joy these youth had when they came up out of the water was almost unexplainable. I had the honor of baptizing my own nephew, Nate. It was quite an experience! Nate said he just couldn't express in words the way he felt! After I left the camp and was driving home through Iowa and Minnesota, I noticed the sky getting blacker and blacker; and as the thunderstorm's fireworks exploded in the sky and lightning flashed out of the heavens, I was reminded of the youth that I had met that day. They are lights in a world that is getting darker and darker.

Matthew 5:16: *In the same way, let your light shine before men, that they may see your good deeds and praise your Father in Heaven.*

It is my hope and prayer that these young people take this excitement for Jesus Christ that they experienced at camp and tip the world upside down with it, which is something that us older folks haven't done yet. To all the youth whom I met on July 4, 2003, at Camp Abe Lincoln, I would like to say this:

Philippians 1:3-6: *I thank my God every time I remember you. In all my prayers for all of you, I always pray with joy because of your partnership in the gospel from the first day until now, being confident of this, that he who began a good work in you will carry it on to completion until the day of Christ Jesus.*

So everyone watch out, because the fuse has been lit!

Your brother in Christ,
George Denn

July 21, 2003

---⊗⊗⊗---

Luke 17:20-21: *Once, having been asked by the Pharisees when the kingdom of God would come, Jesus replied, "The kingdom of God does not come with your careful obser-vation, nor will people say, 'Hereere it is,' or 'There it is,' because the kingdom of God is within you."*

As I look back over the last ten days, three days stand out in my mind. The first of these days happened on a Friday the day Bob, Tim, and myself, all brothers from the same church, decided we would tackle a tree project for Darlene. Little did I know what was in store! As Tim lifted me higher in the bucket of his boom truck, the first thing that happened was the wire for the safety feature broke. Imagine me in a situation where there are no safety features! Guess what I did? I said a prayer as Bob and Tim repaired the wire. Then we moved to the next spot and added an extension to the lift for a total of 120 feet. Up I went again as I tied a rope to a branch and sawed a few limbs, but OOPS! There went the safety feature wire again, but this time they couldn't get the thing fixed; to add to the adventure, the only direction the lift would move was up, and about this time people starting showing up to take pictures of our catastrophe! I am not too good at heights anymore and never was for that matter. I was clutching to a limb, but they needed to raise me higher to take the weight off the boom so it would retract as I went higher and higher.

In desperation I prayed, *God where are you?* I kept remembering Hebrews 13:5 where God says He will never leave us or forsake us.

At that moment I sure felt forsaken, but I was holding on to that promise and the side of the bucket for all I was worth. Those on the ground got a few chuckles at my expense. After I was safely back on the ground and thought about this experience later when I was calmer, I thought how often in life we are stuck in a situation that God tries to move us out of, but like me we are clinging to the tree limb, too scared to move from our perch.

The second memorable day was the following Monday when my nephew, Nate, helped me shock grain bundles on my farm. We were placing barley sheaves together, and I said to him, "Do you know that you can see Jesus in barley sheaves?" He had no idea what I meant and asked me to explain. In Leviticus 23:9-14 it describes how they took the first barley sheaves and waved them in the air as a dedication to the Lord. This was a representation of how one day Jesus would be the first fruit (the best fruit). After I told Nate that, he happily grabbed a sheaf and waved it in the air. As we shocked grain we talked about the parable of the weeds and the wheat (Matthew 13:24-30), which I really appreciated being able to do with my nephew. Then Nate surprised me with a few analogies of his own. He said, "Well, if these sheaves represent people, notice how they need to lean on each other to stand up, and even if they fall over we notice it and pick them up when we get around to that spot. Just like God picks us up when we fall over."

The last memorable day happened on Sunday morning when Nate and I went to help longtime friends clean up debris from a tornado that had struck their farm a week earlier. A lot of cleanup had already taken place before Sunday. I had to laugh a little at a memory; twenty years ago I was over there in the autumn baling corn stalks for this family, and I walked into the shed to get some oil and said to myself, "I am sure glad that I don't have to clean this shed up." Guess what shed I got to help clean up? You guessed it! Does the Lord have a sense of humor or what! As the day progressed two sites were cleared of debris and wreckage. As I drove my skid steer around the farm, I was glad I had come to help the Bade family with the cleanup. If people didn't work together like that it would be nearly impossible to clean up such a mess by yourself, as it would take forever. Also, it was good to talk to people whom I have known almost forever as well as those who I'd just met that day. As we were driving home that afternoon I asked Nate if he had seen the Lord at work today. He said, "Yes! — Just how all the people came together like that to help a family that was in need!"

Acts 20:35: *In everything I did, I showed you that by this kind of hard work we must help the weak, remembering the words The Lord Jesus himself said: "It is more blessed to give than to receive."*

I would have to say this is true, because I have been able to give to others as well as receive, and it is truly a blessing!

Your brother in Christ,
George Denn

August 22, 2003

—⊱⊰—

Luke 15:10: *"In the same way, I tell you, there is rejoicing in the presence of the angels of God over one sinner who repents."*

I just have to write about an interesting person who has recently come into our lives up here in rural Minnesota. Brad Claggett is a gifted twenty-two-year-old musician from Oklahoma; he plays guitar beautifully and has even written some of his own songs. I had the opportunity to hear him play on the way to Chicago where we attended our church conference and later as we drove around the streets of Chicago. There's nothing like having live entertainment! Brad really lives out the exhortation given to us in the following verses from the Psalms:

Psalm 150:1-4: *Praise the Lord. Praise God in his sanctuary; praise him in his mighty heavens. Praise him for his acts of power; praise him for his surpassing greatness. Praise with the sounding of the trumpet, praise him with the harp and lyre, praise him with the tambourine and dancing, praise him with the strings and flute.*

Praising God is something Brad does every chance he can get! My nephew, Nate, met Brad at the S.E.P. Summer camp that they both were part of in June and July. By a strange turn of events Brad ended up in Minnesota living at Nate's home and is now working for me, and I have to say a good time is being had by all.

Psalm 133:1: *How good and pleasant it is when brothers live together in unity!*

As I talked with Brad at the conference one evening, he told me all that he had been through in his young life, and it just touched my heart. How a young person of just twenty-two could have gone through so much already astounded me, and he made the comment that he was surprised he was even still alive! In talking with Brad it made me realize that my life hasn't been as bad as his, and for this I thank God. After we returned home from the conference, Brad confided in me that he had never been baptized, and he wondered if Nate and I could do this for him. I encouraged Brad to let me know when he wanted this done. So at 1:00 pm on August 19, 2003 in the lake right in front of my house where cattle used to cool off and get a drink, we baptized Bradley Wayne Claggett into the fellowship and service of Jesus Christ. It's always an amazing experience to see a person take part in obedience to the plan of God, and to see someone give his life totally to God through the act of baptism knowing that he truly is a son of God through faith in Jesus Christ. Galatians 3:16 - 4:7 and Matthew 11:12 both say that from the days of John the Baptist until now the kingdom of heaven has been forcefully advancing, and forceful men lay hold of it ... men like Brad Claggett.

Your brother in Christ,
George Denn

December 03, 2003

W hen I sit here at my kitchen table and think about the past year, I am amazed at all the things the Lord has done in my life — all the many places He has allowed me to travel to and all the people He has allowed me to meet. I think it is funny how a simple farm boy from south central Minnesota can get to do so many things for the Lord and yet still do what I love best, which is farming. Even better yet, I've been able to write about my experiences. This is very amazing to me!The most recent adventure the Lord allowed me to go on was to the great state of Oklahoma. I've always enjoyed traveling to places where I have never been to before; it's interesting to discover that the images I've conjured up in my mind about a certain place are never the way things really are once I get there. During the last eight days I felt like a stranger in a foreign land, but thanks to the people that I stayed with they made me feel right at home.

Hebrews 13:2 says: *Do not forget to entertain strangers, for by so doing some people have entertained angels without knowing it.*

I am pretty sure that I'm not an angel but if I had been, these folks would have nothing to worry about concerning their obedience to this scripture.

I was traveling with my friend Brad, and our first stop was in Jay, Oklahoma to stay the night with Dave and Theresa Claggett, Brad's dad and stepmother, . About noon the next day we traveled west across Oklahoma through Tulsa and on to Oklahoma City where we spent a few days at the home of Larry and Patty Pope, Brad's mother and stepfather. I got to meet Brad's sister, Lizzy, and his brother Ben and Grandma Ann, but everyone calls her Nene. One day Brad's mother took us to the National Cowboy Hall of Fame, where you can see many artifacts of the American West, from an old west town to the Lone Ranger's mask. They also had a handmade saddle worth $25,000 and Indian artifacts such as an Indian head-dress and a teepee. At night we watched John Wayne movies and a movie about Davy Crockett, and I couldn't help but notice that in all these movies there was a plot of good versus evil just like the plot we are engaged in, called everyday life.

James 1:21: *Therefore, get rid of all moral filth and the evil that is so prevalent and humbly accept the word planted in you, which can save you.*

After a Thanksgiving banquet on Wednesday, we left and headed east once again. As we drove I saw oil wells and cattle everywhere, and I couldn't help but remember the verse in the Ricky Skaggs song, "In the place where I was raised, clocks ticked and the cattle grazed, we all were raised on amazing grace, back where I come from." On through Tulsa and through Claremore, the hometown of Will Rogers, to a town called Vinita where the Claggett family reunion was taking place at the Baptist church there. We enjoyed another Thanksgiving feast, and after that we went to the home of Kermit and Martha Claggett, Brad's grandparents. After a two-day stay and another feast on Friday, we left for Jay, Oklahoma (many thanks again to Kermit and Martha for your hospitality; you made me feel right at home).

On Sunday, David and Theresa took us to Cornerstone Church in Grove, Oklahoma. That afternoon we drove to Arkansas and stopped at a mill along a creek that is powered by a waterwheel; inside was a gift shop where they still grind corn for cornmeal that you can purchase there. Before we left for home, Brad wanted to talk with the youth pastor at the Cornerstone Church. Jim Lay talked with us for two hours. Brad was telling all the things that had happened since he had last talked to Jim. Before we left, Jim and three others prayed for Brad and myself and it was the first time in my life that I was able to witness the gift of tongues. I always wondered what that was like and I know that this can be a controversial subject. I personally do not have this gift, but I know that there are folks in the body of Christ who do have it. (For more on the spiritual gifts read 1 Corinthians chapter 12 through chapter 14.)

As our trip to Oklahoma came to an end, and as we drove the 620 miles home, I thought back on all the wonderful people I had met in Oklahoma as well as all the people I have met in places that I have been to this past year. I started to wonder what the Lord might have in store for me in this coming year. Where will Jesus Christ take me on this journey of life?

1 Corinthians 2:9: *However, as it is written: no eye has seen, no ear has heard, no mind has conceived what God has prepared for those who love him.*

Your brother in Christ,
George Denn

December 18, 2003

<hr>

Isaiah 40:31: *But those who hope in the Lord will renew their strength. They will soar on wings like eagles; they will run and not grow weary, they will walk and not be faint.*

As I stood behind the hearse with the other pallbearers waiting for the family to assemble, someone said look, a bald eagle! I was thinking back to what the minister said in his eulogy of George Sholtz in describing how he accepted Jesus as his Lord and Savior and confessed his belief in him.I was very glad to learn that he had entered into eternal life upon his death, because he had believed on Jesus.

John 3:16: *For God so loved the world that he gave his one and only Son, that whoever believes in him shall not perish but have eternal life.*

It often baffles me how people think they can be good enough to obtain heaven on their own merits or that they are so bad that God wouldn't want them. To this I say phooey!!

Romans 3:22 says: *This righteousness from God comes through faith in Jesus Christ to all who believe. There is no difference, for all have sinned and fall short of the glory of God, and are justified freely by his grace through the redemption that came by Christ Jesus.*

If you dare to read on you will find this is all from God. Anyone alive may have eternal life if he or she wants it. It's all up to the individual, and you will find these facts in the pages of God's Holy Word, the Bible.

As I stood in place with the others at the funeral, my mind drifted through the years that I had known this good man. I was George's neighbor and good friend for forty-one years. Jesus said in Mark 12:31 that the second greatest law was to love your neighbor as yourself. This sums up my neighbor George. I would have been in quite a fix many times in life if God hadn't provided such a good neighbor, and as I stood there I never intended to write about this, but one of the other pallbearers, a man who owns a bar, bought fifty red roses to hand out to the family and pallbearers. As I held the rose I thought how much it reminded me of a person's life. The length of the stem reminded me of the length of one's life, and the bends in the stem reminded me of the twists and turns one encounters on the path of life. The small, leafy branches represent the people who are close to God and depend on Him. Even though the stem of the rose has thorns, there are far more places on the stem that are smooth, but we tend to notice the thorns. This may be a good place to consider Matthew 13:24-30, the Parable of the Weeds. Then I noticed that the stem was smooth with no thorns at all on the last three inches just before the petals; this represents the time when a person makes amends and gets right with God. The red rose itself represents our spiritual body.

1 Corinthians 15:42-44: *So will it be with the resurrection of the dead. The body that is sown is perishable, but it is raised imperishable; it is sown in dishonor, it is raised in Glory; it is sown in weakness, it is raised in power; it is sown a natural body, it is raised a spiritual body.*

Thanks for the roses, Mac; God used you when you made this thoughtful gesture!

Your brother in Christ,
George Denn

January 3, 2004

—◦◦◦◦◦—

2 Corinthians 6:14 - 7:1: *Do not be yoked together with unbelievers. For what do righteousness and wickedness have in common? Or what fellowship can light have with darkness? What harmony is there between Christ and Belial? What does a believer have in common with an unbeliever? What agreement is there between the temple of God and idols? For we are the temple of the living God. As God has said: "I will live with them and walk among them, and I will be their God, and they will be my people. Therefore come out from them and be separate," says the Lord. "Touch no unclean thing, and I will receive you. I will be a Father to you, and you will be my sons and daughters," says the Lord Almighty. Since we have these promises, dear friends, let us purify ourselves from everything that contaminates body and spirit, perfecting holiness out of reverence for God.*

I have just had the privilege of taking part in the winter camp (Snow Blast) that my church sponsors. This year it was held at Camp Omega in Waterville, Minnesota, where we enjoyed three fun and Spirit-filled days . There were about 60 youth ages 10-19 and about 40 workers. My job was assistant counselor in 2B where 14 young men, I believe, ages 14-19 and two other counselors named Jon and Tom bunked for three days and three nights. My other duties, if I could be found, were to help out with whatever needed to be done! I even got to start the bonfire, which was almost an episode of its own! You could really tell God was at work those three days; I don't know who had more of a change, the youth or the adults who were there helping, but I expect it was a little of both! It was great fun — the activities were broomball, capture the flag, snow tubing, dance and arts and crafts. I think the only part of my body where I didn't feel pain was my hair! There were also many spiritual aspects of camp. There were chapel services, skits (I played the part of God in one of them), praise and worship, and classes about Christian living. One of the highlights for me was to see my nephew Zack recommit his life to Christ. The last night we all in dorm 2b laid hands on Zack and prayed for him. The Lord really has His hands on Zack's life. Zack said to me one night during praise and worship that this whole thing was really AWESOME! I said I bet this was the best party he'd ever been to, and he agreed. I also had a niece there named Sara, who said she had a great time as well.

Besides a few minor inconveniences (no water in half the camp for about a day), it was one great experience fellowshipping with other Christians, whether in worship, games, or in discussions that took place. I am reminded of the praise song, "Surely the presence of the Lord is in this place; I can feel His mighty power and His grace. I can hear the brush of angel's wings; I see glory on each face; surely the presence of the LORD is in this place." I can hardly wait for summer camp!

Your brother in Christ,
George Denn

January 27, 2004

⸎

I am always amazed when I see the hand of God working in a mighty way in my life! No more so than this past weekend. I took my two nephews Nate and Zack to a youth get-together in Orr, Minnesota. Tom Kennebeck (nicknamed Ted) and Tom Burnett were hosting. I slid down hills, got snow in my face, drank hot chocolate, ate chili, hauled firewood, and even rode down a water slide that evening in the hotel. It took me about five times down to figure out how to slide down the thing which seems extremely funny to two individuals whose identity will remain forever a secret, but you know who You are! Finally some young guy told me what to do and then it was almost too easy!The next day, Sunday, we worshiped in the Lutheran Church in Orr. It's interesting to experience two congregations worshiping together; you could just feel the presence of the Holy Spirit there. I played the part of God again in a skit, and I got to dispense the gifts of forgiveness, unconditional love, and eternal life to three people who were captured by materialism, drugs, and pornography. I just sent Jesus to rescue them from these things that the devil had them under bondage! I also had the opportunity to listen to another friend of mine, Gordy Lindquist, as he gave the message. He talked about David and Goliath and asked us to think about the Goliath in our life (mine is finances; they are always growling at me). And how Jesus tells us in our daily lives and the choices we make to chose life! As we split up and went home I left totally inspired and totally glad we had come…

I remember when Tom Kennebeck has asked us to come up he said they would spring for the gas money to get there, and they were relying on Christ to come up with the money. I told him not to worry about it at all because the Lindquists had invited us, and so we were coming up that way anyway. As I've retraced my steps on this journey, I've been thinking a lot about the scripture in Matthew 6 verses 19-24 (about having your treasures in heaven) and Matthew 6 verses 25-34, for I have a sermon coming up myself. Anyway, I counted the money that I had for the trip, which was $305, I bought two pounds of beef jerky at Hilltop Meat Market for around $34; I filled my gas tank once going up for about $30, plus coffee and treats for the way home. Gordy filled my gas tank coming home.

When I returned home I needed to make my truck loan payment, so I counted the money that I had left over from the trip. I figured I had spent between $70 and $100 for the three-day trip, but I wanted to count it to see what I really had left, and if it would be enough for my truck payment. Well, I counted the money and found that I still had $294! I counted it again, and yes, it was still $294. I counted it a third time — $294. How did Jesus do this? I don't know how He did it. How did He feed the 5000 people in John chapter 6? I can't explain it; I can only believe it just as I believe the story in the Bible! Many people tried to give explanations for what had happened — that I had counted wrong; that I had counted twice before I left; that someone had slipped some money into my billfold when I wasn't looking. It would have been kind of hard for someone to do that as I had it with me most of the time except at night when I was sleeping! I will claim as John did to Peter in John 21 verse 7, "It is the Lord!" Eleven dollars spent on a 600-mile, three-day trip! So Tom, the Lord did provide the gas money after all!

Your friend in Christ,
George Denn

February 26, 2004

—∞—

Isaiah 52:14: *Just as there were many who were appalled at him — his appearance was so disfigured beyond that of any man and his form marred beyond human likeness.*

I just returned home after watching the movie "The Passion of the Christ" by Mel Gibson with my nephews Dustin, Zack, and Nate, and all I can say is that finally we have an accurate description of what Jesus Christ went through (although in reality His crucifixion was probably a lot worse). As I sat there watching the movie, I was thinking of all the controversies surrounding this movie. That's pretty typical; most people can handle the concept of God pretty well, but put Jesus in the equation and you have controversy, because Jesus was a controversial God/man (that alone is controversial!). As a matter of fact, Jesus said in **Luke 12:51:** *"Do you think I came to bring peace on earth? No, I tell you, but division."* The following verses go on to describe how a lot of times the division is within one's own family. Jesus' message is a spiritual one; He said many times those that have an ear (for what He is talking about) let them hear. One cannot really know Jesus and what He is talking about unless one reads about this Jesus in Matthew, Mark, Luke, and John in the Bible.

As I sat there watching Jesus first getting hit with the end of what I would call a log chain, then stripped and handcuffed to a large block of wood; beaten with sticks and then with whips that tore the skin, I was thinking of some of the critics of this movie who had said things like, "Way too much blood and gore" and "Overdone with beatings!" What a lie from Satan. The reality was probably far worse than the movie depicted, and these same people when they were younger most likely sat through movies such as the "Texas Chainsaw Massacre" and probably didn't have a problem with it! It is to Satan's advantage to make the sufferings of Jesus Christ less than they actually were! WE all are so used to seeing these puny Jesus figures hanging limply on a cross.

I'm looking at one now! A little guy about 125-150 pounds maybe; cut on one side; a few drops of blood; sad face. We come from a society that likes to cover up the truth! Why not let the younger people see this movie? Maybe then it won't take them so long to understand what Jesus Christ did for them! Then they won't have to suffer years of sinful lifestyles and broken lives like some of us older folks have gone through because Jesus Christ wasn't real to us. I say that because I am one of those people.

Also there is talk of this movie causing anti-Semitism ... but that's only if God is left out of the picture! It was God Who killed Jesus, for that was His sole purpose for coming down here to earth in the first place. As long as there were people, Jesus had to die to redeem them.

Galatians 3:13: *Christ redeemed us from the curse of the law by becoming a curse for us, for it is written: "Cursed is everyone who is hung on a tree."*

As Jesus was nailed to the cross and blood was flowing everywhere, those doing this to Him weren't too careful about it because in their thinking, why should they be? They figured he was going to die anyway. He had to be God, because no earthly man could live through all that! Jesus knew He had to get to that cross, because if He didn't, Satan would have won!

John 16:11: *And in regard to judgment, because the prince of this world now stands condemned.*

The movie ends with Jesus getting up and walking out of the tomb. He has gained victory over death and is alive!

Well, I encourage everyone to go and see this movie because I believe it was God who inspired Mel Gibson to make it, and there is no way you will be the same person after watching it as you were before! Like the tough Roman centurion who was sitting on his horse when the sky turned black and the ground shook and split open, I am sure you'll be convinced that SURELY THIS WAS THE SON OF GOD (Matthew 27:54)!

Your brother in Christ,
George Denn

March 30, 2004

––––⊙⊙⊙––––

Hosea 10:12: *Sow for yourselves righteousness, reap the fruit of unfailing love, and break up your unplowed ground; for it is time to seek the Lord, until he comes and showers righteousness on you.*

I was looking out the window at my walking plow that I use for a lawn ornament, and thought it was perfect for my story. But being cold out today I brought it into my house to prop my feet on while I write! Mom used to say that someday I'd bring a tractor into the house, but so far this is the closest I have come to doing that! One time I had it in church near the podium as I gave the sermon, so you might say this is my sacred plow! It is finally springtime, which comes late to Minnesota, and so I thought I would just ask God to help me write a story of springtime renewal, the time for plowing and for sowing the seeds. I want to mention some things about plowing for those who don't know much about it, even though we don't do much plowing anymore because of modern machinery. But in the days when we plowed, there was nothing easy about it! Plowing used to be one-third of the work done on a farm to produce a crop. This old plow that my feet are perched on was once pulled by two horses with the leather lines around your neck and under your arm so as to free up your hands to guide your plow and team of horses, and if you hit a stone, you were sent flying over the handle bars; keep in mind you still had those leather lines around your neck! Back and forth and back and forth all day long walking behind your plow – it was slow and steady work. Then riding plows came on the scene; these were hitched to three to twelve horses, usually in teams, three horses abreast depending on soil conditions. The harder the soil, the more horses you needed. Same leather lines around your neck and under your arm to free up your hands to guide your team and run the plow, but with the riding plow if you hit a stone you got tipped over and sent flying into the plowed ground with those lines still tied around your neck and under your arms ... back and forth, back and forth across the field all day long. Then finally someone invented the tractor. In my youth I remember running alongside the tractor late in the fall just to keep warm. This was before tractors had cabs. About the time plowing became fairly easy as far as comfort goes, farmers quit using them because they'd been replaced with faster implements. Also in the springtime the soil turns easier than in the fall ... young people, hold that thought! As this great nation moved westward, it was axes and plows that built the nation and my family was part of this process to break the land to feed a nation and then to feed the world.

As I look at my own life, I want you to consider yours. For those of you who know the Lord Jesus Christ, what unplowed ground is in your life that you haven't yet plowed and broken up for the kingdom of God? Those of you who know the Lord is calling you, what will it take to plow up the ground to get you where God wants you to be? For those of you who haven't a clue to what I am talking about, don't worry, you will someday.

Romans 14:11-12: *It is written: "As surely as I live, says the Lord, every knee will bow before me; every tongue will confess to God." So then, each of us will give an account of himself to God.*

The Lord has made me aware of the unplowed ground in my life as well as the soil conditions hardened by years of neglect. There is a saying that I've always liked: "Do whatever it takes to get the job done." So it is with farming; if we don't get the soil in condition to sow the seeds in the springtime, neither will we have a harvest in the fall! We would starve and so would the world if all farmers would just do nothing when it was high time to be out in the fields!

What will the grain bins of our lives look like? Aren't you curious? I sure am, for that is when our work down here will take on the most meaning.

> **1 Peter 1:24:** *For, All men are like grass, and all their glory is like the flowers of the field; the grass withers and the flowers fall but the word of the Lord stands forever.*

And this is the word that was preached to you!
Your brother in Christ,
George Denn

April 13, 2004

—∞—

Matthew 6:26: *Look at the birds of the air; they do not sow or reap or store away in barns, and yet your heavenly father feeds them. Are you not much more valuable than they?*

Yesterday Troy Peterson, Brad Claggett, and I took off to go look at a pickup that was for sale. I've been praying for one to use here on the farm here, as my little Dodge Dakota wasn't made for farm work. I've also been praying for a planter to plant pumpkins with. I kept having visions of last year. It took three of us a week to plant 18 acres! Then we had to replant because of striped gophers digging up all the seeds. God bless those little buggers, they like pumpkins too! ... the seeds, that is. Anyway, Troy said, "You know, George, Dad has an old corn planter at our place." I said, "Troy, why didn't you have this brainstorm last year?" He looked puzzled for a minute and then replied, "I guess I just didn't think of it,". That's about how I operate too! We went to look at it and it was perfect in every way, and best of all, it was free. Marlin Peterson wouldn't take a cent for it. I called my friend Jeff and asked, "Can you haul this thing for me?" He said he'd be glad to. I called Jim Anderson and asked, "Can I use your trailer Jim?" "Yes!" I'm starting to understand Matthew 6:26 a little better as I see how perfectly God provides for me! Jesus tells us that in this life one needs to watch the birds to understand how we should trust God for our provision. Birds tend to gather in flocks; they swoop down to the ground and eat food that is already there; they use materials for their homes that are absolutely free. No stores, no fast foods, no credit cards, no debts, NO worries!

Now I have to ask, who are the smart ones here? I think it's the ones with the feathers!

Just as the birds gather together in flicks, so were we three buddies together yesterday when the idea for the planter was formed. Then another "bird," Marlin Peterson, had this old planter that was just sitting in his yard for a long, long time. Two other "birds" that flock together, Jeff and Jim, helped me with their pickup and trailer. Another "bird," Jennie Peterson, Marlin's wife, was happy to see it leave her yard, but even happier it could still be used for something yet! If you add all these "birds" up they turn into quite a flock that is singing quite a song of happiness together!

Matthew 6:19-21: *Do not store up for yourselves treasures on earth, where moth and rust destroy, and where thieves break in and steal. But store up for yourselves treasures in heaven, where moth and rust do not destroy, and where thieves do not break in and steal. For where your treasure is, there your heart will be also.*

Ever since day one my pumpkins have been dedicated to the Lord's work, and every year the Lord does some extraordinary things with these pumpkins! I have no idea how many lives these pumpkins have touched or will continue to touch. It keeps getting bigger every year!

Now this old planter is full of rust, and probably the only person who would steal it would be one who deals in scrap iron. At one time this planter was quite a purchase. But seventy years later it is basically worthless for the work for which it was once designed. The little life this old planter has left in it will be used for God's purposes, and if any lives are changed and come to know Jesus Christ as their Lord and Savior because of its use, then the benefits are eternal and there is no human price tag on that!

Mark 4:30-32: *Again he said, "What shall we say the kingdom of God is like, or what parable shall we use to describe it? It is like a mustard seed, which is the smallest seed you plant in the ground. Yet when planted, it grows* *and becomes the largest of all garden plants, with such big branches that the birds of the air can perch in its shade."*

Yep, the kingdom of God ... there is nothing to compare, and I am one "bird" who is glad I found it, and so will you!

Your brother in Christ,
George Denn

June 2, 2004

⎯⎯⎯∞⎯⎯⎯

Psalm 19:1-4: *The heavens declare the glory of God; the skies proclaim the work of his hands. Day after day they pour forth speech; night after night they display knowledge. There is no speech or language where their voice is not heard. Their voice goes out into all the earth, their words to the ends of the world.*

A week ago, I and four others, Jeff and Troy Peterson, Brad Claggett, and Mark Rummel took a few days off from our regular routine and headed to Northern Minnesota to the little town of Orr on the east side of Pelican Lake. We stayed on the west side of Pelican Lake in a small cabin that is owned by our friends, Tom and Jenny Burnett. Even though this place had no electricity or running water, it was the best place I have stayed at while fishing as far as comfort! It was still fairly spring-like weather up there. A lot of the trees still had no leaves and the water was still ice cold. We caught Northern Pike, Largemouth Bass and Jumbo Perch in the day and had deep spiritual conversations in the evenings … the kind that we never seem to have time for when talking after church. After a time we all could see there was a reason that we were there! As we talked about God and to God and allowed God to talk to us, there was a great peace that surrounded the place. We had a bonfire outside, and even though each log was burning in a different way, they all burned together to create one giant flame. As I looked above the fire, I saw sparks flying skyward. I thought of **Job 5:7:** *Yet man is born to* *trouble as surely as sparks fly upward.* The next morning when I got up and went outside I noticed four logs that had been separated from the rest of the fire and were barely smoldering! God really spoke to me through those logs.

I had the opportunity to talk to the man whom Tom had bought his cabin from. I was curious how the town of Orr got its name. Aman by the name of Billy Orr started a store there to sell merchandise to the logging camp. His motto was NO CHURCHES IN ORR! I thought that was interesting. Logging camps in the early 1900s were pretty rough and raw! As we left we decided to stop by Tom's house and say goodbye. As you enter Orr from the south there is a sign that says, "Welcome to Orr, Home of the Giant Blue Gill". In some ways this was like a trip back in time for Brad and Mark because they attended the church camp that once was located near Orr on Pelican Lake. So they wanted to get their picture taken by the sign. As Brad and Mark stood by the fish against the sign, I noticed the 't' for the word 'to' was superimposed between Brad and Mark and it looked like a big cross! A fish and a cross, two Christian symbols that say Jesus Christ is alive and well in the town of Orr in spite of the founder's motto! As long as there are men like Tom Burnett and Tom Kennebeck and their families living there, He always will be!

Psalm 19:14: May the words of my mouth and the meditation of my heart be pleasing in your sight, O Lord, my Rock and my Redeemer.

Your brother in Christ,
  George Denn

July 30, 2004

Ecclesiastes 2:17: *So I hated life, because the work that is done under the sun was grievous to me. All of it is meaningless, a chasing after the wind. I hated all the things I had toiled for under the sun, because I must leave them to the one who comes after me.*

As I am riding in my pickup to our Christian S. E. P. summer camp (spiritual enhancement program), where I will participate in as a worker this year, my nephew Nate is driving and it will take us seven hours to get there, so this gives me a chance to write this story. This year it looked like God was giving me a window of opportunity to be a worker at camp as it was scheduled for August 1-7. I figured small grain harvest would be done with by then like it has been for years, but my plans for a fairly smooth summer came to an end as did the drought we were having on June 8th when we received nine inches of rain in one night! It rained almost nonstop till after July 4th. Doing seven weeks' worth of work in just three and a half weeks was not what I had in mind when I'd committed myself to camp! **Proverbs 20:24** says, *A mans steps are directed by the Lord. How than can anyone understand his own way?* Believe me, I was trying to understand! Somehow I knew things would turn out just fine, but there were many days when all I had to hold onto was that thought. The last week arrived and I still had 245 acres of hay, oats, and wheat to harvest, as well as straw to bale and 70 acres to plant back for a fall hay crop!

I had faith that God would act, but my faith was starting to wear a bit thin by this time. What does it mean to have faith?

Hebrews 11:1-2: *Now faith is being sure of what we hope for and certain of what we do not see. This is what the ancients were commended for.*

Yep, my faith was wearing pretty thin, and I just want to thank all of those who were praying for me at this time, because I couldn't have done it without your help! There were so many things that just came together on the last few days that only God could have helped me with. On Monday a fellow by the name of Allen and his partner Dale were looking to buy some straw, and they were interested in buying 56 acres' worth. I was telling Allen what I was up against and he said "George, you can erase that much from your mind"! But by Thursday, my last day before leaving for the trip to camp, 22 acres of it reappeared; perhaps I didn't use a big enough eraser! Some bales were getting hot from being baled to soon!

It is now 3 o'clock in the afternoon the day before I leave, and I have one more load of straw to bale and 30 acres left to seed, and I see Dale and Allen coming across the field to talk. I'm really wondering if I should stop and talk to these two or if I should just keep baling. Well, they had bad news for me — they had planned to move those bales off the field so I could at least get it seeded, but said they just couldn't do it! Dale mentioned he didn't think this kind of thing would bother me after reading all my articles that I have written over the years. Do you know what a rubber band looks like just before it snaps? I'm sure I looked just like that because I sure felt like it!

But after they left I asked Jesus for help, because there was just too much work left to do and not enough time to do it! I called my neighbor David Hiniker, and he hauled my skid steer to the field and I removed the bales. We started planting at 7 o'clock and I finished a 10:15 in the evening, just in time to fall into bed for a good night's sleep before the road trip.

Luke 8:15: *But the seed on good soil stands for those with a noble and good heart, who hear the word, retain it, and by persevering produce a crop.*

The closer we get to the camp, the more I can sense that I truly persevered!

Your friend in Christ,
George Denn

August 8, 2004

—⊶—

Psalm 84:10-12: *Better is one day in your courts than a thousand elsewhere; I would rather be a doorkeeper in the house of my God than dwell in the tents of the wicked. For the Lord God is a sun and a shield; the Lord bestows favor and honor; no good thing does he withhold from those whose walk is blameless. O Lord Almighty, blessed is the man who trusts in you.*

After returning home from being one of the staff at S. E. P. camp, all I can say is WOW! For nine days I shut off my cell phone and refused to have any contact with the outside world. For nine days my stress level was running at about zero and I had very little use for money except to buy an occasional pop. I was able to experience a place that was as close to heaven as I have ever been! I was in charge of overnight tent camping and a nature hike in which we focused on the Parable of the Four Soils in Luke 8:4-18. I am not sure who learned more, the campers or me, but I expect it was some of both! Also, along with supervising the tent camping I helped with building fires, hauling wood, and cooking hamburgers and hotdogs for the campers. One of the leaders of the camp, our District Superintendent, David Fiedler, mentioned one night that these young people need to see Jesus living in us camp leaders, but that there is also another side of the coin, which is that we need to see Jesus in them. I have to admit at times that was tough. But nonetheless, if you looked you could see Him. Just like the Parable of the

Fishing Net in Matthew 13:47-52 we had a camp full of attitudes, some good and some bad, and believe me, some were pretty bad!

But all in all, the good purpose that we had gathered there for prevailed, and like a well-oiled machine with every part working each of us was placed and allowing Jesus to work through us, about 100 out of the 130 campers asked Jesus Christ into their hearts and lives as Lord and Savior or recommitted their lives once again, and eight of these young people were baptized into the service of Jesus Christ! On the last day of camp, the youth challenged the staff in games.

While I was in the horseshoe–pitching area, I asked Brian, a fifteen-year-old who was to be baptized, why a young person such as himself would gravitate towards drugs and alcohol; he told me, "there is no hope out there for young people." Could it be possible that as we are going along on the path of life we are somehow forgetting that Jesus Christ gives us REAL LIFE ... meaning, not the things that money can buy.

Luke 12:15: *Watch out! Be on your guard against all kinds of greed; a man's life does not consist in the abundance of his possessions.*

John 10:10: The thief comes only to STEAL and KILL and DESTROY; I have come that they may have life, and have it to the full.

1 Timothy 6:10: *For the love of money is a root of all kinds of evil. Some people, eager for money, have wandered from the faith and pierced themselves with many griefs.*

Thankfully we have a Savior who can redeem the time we have spent chasing worthless idols like money, drugs, alcohol, illicit sex, and so on. His name is Jesus Christ, the only Son of God, and He is alive and well and lives in the hearts and lives of those who have asked Him in.

Revelation 22:14-15: *Blessed are those who have washed their robes, that they may have the right to the tree of life and may go through the gates into the city. Outside are the dogs those who practice magic arts the sexually immoral, the murderers, the idolaters and everyone who loves and practices falsehood.*

So in closing I am grateful to have met some old friends and some new friends; it truly was a rewarding nine days.

Revelation 22:21: *The grace of the Lord Jesus be with God's people. Amen*

Your brother in Christ,
George Denn

November 19, 2004

Isaiah 12:4-5: *In that day you will say: Give thanks to the Lord, call on his name; make known among the nations what he has done, and proclaim that his name is exalted. Sing to the Lord, for he has done glorious things; Let this be known to all the world.*

Thanksgiving will be here in week, and I have been pondering in my mind and heart about the things I am thankful for. A lot of different things that I am unthankful for try to steal away my attention, so I find myself really having to concentrate on the things that I am thankful for. In doing so I realize that some of the things that happened to me this past year, which at the time seemed to be things I was unthankful for, really turned out to be blessings in disguise! In the fall after harvest time is over a farmer tends to reflect on the year he has had, and in this past year I've been stretched so far in certain areas of my life that I feel like that toy Stretch Armstrong. I don't know if he is still around or not. I'm sure some of you remember him! Never have I been stretched and tested like I have this past year. Some of you who know me well are probably thinking I say that every year! So I'm just going to jot down some of the things that I am thankful for. As I write these down and as you read them, hopefully you will consider the things in your own life that you are thankful for.First I am thankful for the church I attend, and I am thankful for everyone who attends there, for I know each person well and they know me. I am thankful to have been part of two Christian youth camps and a canoe trip, for I did not have those opportunities when I was younger. I am thankful to have seen so many young people give there lives to Jesus Christ this past year, and hopefully that will come to fruition in their lives and they won't spend countless years in worthless pursuits. I am thankful for the many places that I have been, and all the friends from all over I have come to know. I am thankful for all my friends who have passed away this past year, because God used them to shape my life. I am thankful for my dad, who is still the best friend I have! I am thankful for friendships that were healed, for I know that it was only Christ who could have done that! I am thankful for all the people who will read this book, for this is something God has given me to do. I am thankful to be a farmer. Although there isn't much money to be had in this profession, I always manage to have a lot of fun! Also, this farm is a place where I see God, Jesus, and the Holy Spirit at work every day!

> **Acts 17:24-27:** *The God who made the world and everything in it is the Lord of Heaven and Earth and does not live in temples built by hands. And he is not served by human hands as if he needed anything, because he himself gives all men life and breath and everything else. From one man He made every nation of men, that they should inhabit the whole earth; and he determined the times set for them and the exact places where they should live. God did this so men would seek him and perhaps reach out for him and find him, though he is not far from each one of us.*

WOW! Now that is something to be thankful for!

Your brother in Christ,
George Denn

P.S. — A special thanks to my long-time friend Julie Sieberg, who encouraged me greatly yesterday morning, for without that some of this could have not been written! I can tell God is alive and well on the Sieberg farm also! The Lord sure does work in mysterious ways.

February 22, 2005

—❧—

Proverbs 16: 9: *In his heart a man plans his course but the Lord determines his steps.*

This past weekend my church sponsored its annual winter mini-camp called "Snow Blast". I had been looking forward to the weekend for some time, and I thought I probably wouldn't have much to do so it was just going to be a laid-back weekend. I was even giving Doug Johannsen a rough time. I'll just call him the guy in charge and I hope I spelled his name right or he will get me somewhere else down the road! Anyway, when he came up with Plan B because of no snow, I asked him what Plan C was, and he said, "We don't want to go there!" I was telling Doug that if he needed one, commotions were my specialty!**Psalm 37:13:** *But the Lord laughs at the wicked, for he knows there day is coming.* When I showed up on Saturday and received my responsibilities for the weekend, I found out I was counselor for group C boys aged 14-18. My first thought was, *wait a minute — I said that I was good at creating commotions, not taking care of them*! As we experienced the first day's activities, Broom Ball and the Orienteering Challenge course, I noticed some interesting points that kept surfacing. Also, to redeem myself in the eyes of some, the fact that I was along when they created the course and that my team won had absolutely no connection whatsoever! I was very surprised that we won because I fell three times on the ice and messed up my arm, and our score wasn't all that high. I like to think it was all just Satan's futile attempt to make me look bad!

After our bonfire sing along and two hours' worth of games, it was time for the dorm chat. This is where those of us who are counselors try to bring the youth into a discussion about Jesus Christ by using the day's events to explain why they need him in their lives in the first place! This would be the equivalent of taking a bunch of wild lions and training them to sit at your feet and then being able to pet them and say nice kitty! It may not be quite that bad but close, real close! I knew without the help of God Almighty this just wasn't going to happen! I and the three other counselors wanted to make some sort of impact on this group, as that was what we were all here for, so we prayed HARD! After about 45 minutes trying , my fellow counselors Steve, James, Theodore and I finally got Steven, Josh, Ky, RJ, Elliot, Isaac, and Teshome settled down for our talk.

I was amazed that we were able to keep our talk Christ–centered, at least on the counselors' end, and I could see the Holy Spirit at work in the boys' hearts. All in all I believe the weekend was a great success, even though a couple of times I felt like getting into my pickup and driving away, but I'm more in charge of my feelings than I used to be, and we did get some snow! But it was wet snow, and the tubers seemed like they had more fun coming up the towrope than sliding down the hill!

I have to take a moment to tell about Isaac, who was from Chicago via Milwaukee. He wore a do-rag and black hat shifted so the brim was sideways on his head, and his prized possession was a blue earring that he referred to as his "eye!" A couple words he liked to use were "clean and fresh." Everything had to be clean and fresh for Isaac or he wouldn't participate — hair, body, clothes, shoes, all had to be FRESH! I know as long as I live whenever I hear the words clean or fresh I will think of Isaac. I asked Isaac what he thought of Jesus Christ, and his reply was, "man, Jesus is the most hip dude around." I changed a word there for safety! "Ain't nobody like Jesus, but I'm just not ready to follow Him yet!" I can relate to Isaac very well, because there was a time in my life when I wasn't ready. Jesus won't let a person stay in that position very long, though, because like Isaac, Jesus Christ likes everything clean and fresh! Without Him in our hearts and lives we just can't have that.

John 3:18-21: *Whoever believes in him is not condemned, but whoever does not believe stands condemned already because he has not believed in the name of God's one and only Son. This is the verdict: Light has come into the world, but men loved darkness instead of light because their deeds were evil. Everyone who does evil hates the light, and will not come into the light for fear that his deeds will be exposed. But whoever lives by the truth comes into the light, so that it may be seen plainly that what he has done has been done through GOD.*

So it really is a choice that only we can make, and Isaac, I hope that "FRESH" New Bible helps you to truly follow Jesus and to really understand what it means to be "CLEAN and FRESH!

Your brother in Christ,
George Denn

June 25, 2005

—⚬⚭⚬—

Joshua 1:9: *Have I not commanded you? Be strong and courageous. Do not be terrified do not be discouraged; for the Lord your God will be with you wherever you go.*

Soon I will leave the familiar fields of southern Minnesota, a place that I would call my comfort zone, to take a journey to northern Minnesota and go to places where I've never been before in a canoe on an adventure called Servant's Passage; the purpose of this journey is to seek God and to be closer to Him and to those who serve Him. I will leave some of my work for when I return, and some of the work that can't wait I will leave in the hands of others to do while I am gone. I'm feeling a little hesitant about doing this in a year that has already been plagued by too much rain and a tornado that hit my farm. For a couple of weeks I was wondering if I should go at all, but I tend to commit myself to these trips and make my life fit around them. I thought it would be a fun thing to document my experiences with the Lord and with others as they unfold. So here we go …Sunday I was asked to give the message at the Orr church. One of the ways I saw God working in my life. A year ago I found out that the founder of Orr, Minnesota had a motto of "No Churches in Orr." He was sure that churches would ruin his business of ill repute. However I noticed his picture hanging in the room of the municipal building where the Worldwide Church of God meets. So it is funny to me that Billy Orr's picture is hanging in a place that he didn't want in his own town! I am reminded of **Psalm 14:1:** *The fool says in his heart there is no God, they are corrupt by their deeds are vile there is no one who does good.* Who knows if Billy Orr didn't find Jesus in the end, because that is what really counts! So I can't wait till tomorrow to see something from God.

Monday we started paddling canoes; there were twenty-seven of us in all. We started at Crane Lake and canoed for about eighteen miles to a place called My Island, where we camped for the night. Our canoe seemed to be the slowest one all day. It is interesting to see the human element come out in us when things are going less than perfect, and I ended up having to say I was sorry to Brad for some of the words that flew out of my mouth! Just to see people bonding with each other and the fact that we paddled eighteen miles in a canoe without dropping over is how I saw God working in my life today. Following Jesus is not for the faint at heart, and I have to admit sometimes that I can be pretty faint at heart.

Psalm 62:1-2: *My soul finds rest in God alone; My salvation comes from him. He alone is my rock and salvation he is my fortress I will never be shaken.*

Tuesday started with breakfast and much eagerness on my part for the trip to begin. We traveled about seven miles by canoe and had a half-mile portage that reminded me of a giant cow path. Mud so thick that it took some shoes off, and I had to walk barefoot while packing our equipment. Good thing there was some Poison Ivy for traction in some places (I am being sarcastic here!).

Some places we were in mud up to our knees, and we were all very thankful to get through that; it was about as close to hell as I ever want to get! The day ended with a great place to camp and we had some breakout sessions. I had no tent that evening. I prayed that God would take away the mosquitoes. As soon as I'd finished praying, Tom told me there was room in a tent and only six people had to sleep under the stars.

Isaiah 40:29-31: *He gives strength to the weary and increases the power of the weak. Even youths grow tired and weary;*

and young men stumble and fall; but those who hope in the Lord will renew their strength. They will soar on wings like eagles; they will run and not grow weary, they will walk and not be faint.

Wednesday when we woke up the scenery looked so picturesque it could have been in one those Hamm's beer commercials minus the beer of course. We broke camp, paddled another seven miles, and made camp again. Today an eighteen-year-old named Josh decided that he would be baptized into the fellowship of Jesus Christ. We were out on this huge rock and a deer walked right through our camp and out by the water less than 200 feet from us. After Josh was baptized, some of us went fishing. I prayed that we would catch a lot of fish, and we caught over seventy, so this was another day of seeing God's hand in a great way. When I saw the deer I was reminded of **Psalm 42:1-2:** *As the deer pants for streams of water so my soul pants Oh God my soul thirsts for God, for the living God. When can I go and meet with the living God?*

Thursday we had the opportunity to spend one hour seeking God. As everyone left the campfire I stayed right where I was! As I was looking at the fire I thought, *LORD, I feel like those logs in the fire – useless;* but then I saw God in the fire and he reminded me that burning logs do keep people warm, so I asked God to just consume me as He did the logs in the fire. Then I saw two pair of shoes smoking; they were Ben and John's tennis shoes that were just starting to burn, so I moved them out of harm's way. God showed me that sometimes I notice things that others don't always see. Next, I threw a log on the fire that others had been using to sit on, and God showed me that the unique ministry He has given me is that I am able to do things that I wouldn't be able to do if I was involved with another's ministry. As I sat there silently, John showed up by the fire and Denise also, and I thought how God works through other people, so I prayed for them. Then I thought, *I am neither married nor do I have material wealth, and I thank God for every trial in life that has brought me to this place in time. I cannot do any thing that our triune God asks of me unless I am empowered by the Holy Spirit.*

I really need to seek Father God, Jesus Christ, and the Holy Spirit in a more complete way.

Then I looked to the sky above and saw three seagulls flying one behind the other as God confirmed my thoughts. **Jeremiah 29:13-14:** *You will seek me and find me when you seek me with all your heart I will be found by you declares the Lord.*

Thanks, Doug, for the use of your pen so that I could capture these thoughts and the words God spoke to my heart while they're fresh in my mind. As we returned from our canoe trip and then drove home, I know that the lives of each of us who went on this journey will be forever changed! I have never spent a week in such a remote place.

I wonder how we will act once we get back to electricity? My only prayer is that we don't all go back to everyday life and take up right where we left off, without taking the things that we learned on this journey and letting God change us as well as the way we live our everyday lives.

> **Mark 10:29-31:** *"I tell you the truth," Jesus replied, "No one has left home or brothers or sisters or mothers or father or children or fields for me and the gospel will fail to receive a hundred times as much in this present age (homes, brothers, sisters, mothers, children and fields with persecutions) and in the age to come, eternal life, but many who are first will be last and the last first."*

Your brother in Christ,
George Denn

August 9, 2005

───∞∞∞───

Psalm 145:3-6: *Great is the Lord and most worthy of praise; his greatness no one can fathom. One generation will commend your words to another they will tell of your mighty acts. They will speak of the glorious splendor of your majesty, and I will meditate on your wonderful works. They will tell of the power of your awesome works and I will proclaim your great deeds.*

A couple of days ago I returned home from S.E.P camp. My duties were to be the assistant counselor to the boys in dorm 2B ages 12-14 and anything else that could be found for me to do, at first anyway, but due to the rambunctious nature of the eighteen boys in our dorm I was allowed to settle into my role as assistant counselor with nothing more expected of me! It sure was most enjoyable! Once again I turned off my cell phone, and the Eagle's Crest camp in Lacon, Illinois was my world for one week. My stress level just deflated like an inner tube with a hole in it! The first day's activities included paint ball. I know I really enjoyed it! I had this camper from 1B whom I'll just call Mr. D from 1B, because he always referred to me as Mr. George! Mr. D is about 4 feet tall and weighs about 65 pounds. Mr. D told me that he was going to take me out in paint ball! I just laughed, but he really did take me out! Our theme this year was EXTREME MAKEOVER, which God has to do for us after the EXTREME TAKEOVER by Satan of mankind in the Garden of Eden (Genesis 3).

We had chapel service every day and after that we had the opportunity to go back to the dorms and talk to the boys and ask them their thoughts on the day's theme. On Wednesday Brad was asked to give his testimony about how he came to know and follow Jesus Christ. After that the boys really opened up. I tell you, some of their stories would just rip your heart right out! It makes me wonder what has happened to our world since I was a kid! Sometimes I felt as if I had woken up on another planet.

On Wednesday we went to a high ropes challenge course, which was my very first time on one of these. The boys had to hook themselves to some overhead cables with some straps and walk across a log suspended in air across what looked like several rope swings and another cable that was thirty feet in the air; they tried to tight-rope across this while holding on to a cable that was over their heads, and at the end of that they had to climb twenty more feet into the tree where they were hooked to a zip line and sent cruising 300 feet down the hill! I pretty much had made up my mind that I wasn't going to do the challenge course, but then Mr. D from 1B asked Mr. George aren't you going to do the course? At the risk of being called chicken man for the rest of camp, I decided to show these boys I could do this without dying of fright! About halfway through the course I was thinking that maybe being called chicken man wouldn't be so bad after all! As you can see, though, I lived through it and was able to write about it!

On Wednesday evening we had a water balloon fight, and Mr. D from 1B came up to me and said "Mr. George, you are going down." I of course laughed at this statement, but on the fifth round Mr. D snuck up behind me and POW got me with a balloon, and I was taken down! As the week progressed we could really see the Holy Spirit working in the boys' hearts, and in our dorm there were six boys interested in being baptized, which was amazing because our dorm seemed to have the most boys who wanted to kill one another! I just figured this was a spiritual issue against the purposes we all were there for teaching them about Jesus Christ and what He has done for us if we choose to accept it (John 3:16 & 17).

After the baptisms and when camp was over, I came upon a young fellow whose name is Isaac. If you recall I wrote about him last winter. I asked Isaac why he hadn't gotten into the pool (referring to baptism), and he said he just wasn't quite ready yet, but I could tell he wasn't the same person he had been last winter; a definite change had taken place in him in the last six months! I asked him where his earring went. He had always referred to it as his "eye." Isaac said that he was messing around with that book I had sent him (meaning he was reading the Bible I had sent him) and the earring "just didn't glorify God." I also told him not to be afraid to follow Jesus, and that I had been doing so for ten years now and hadn't regretted one second of it! Of all the things that went on at camp, my conversation with Isaac was the best part of all, for God showed me how He had used me to touch another person's life!

Isaiah 55:8-11: *As the Heavens are higher than the earth so are my ways higher than your ways and my thoughts higher than your thoughts. As the rain and the snow come down from heaven, and do not return to it without watering the earth and making it bud and flourish so that it yields seed for the sower and bread for the eater, so is my word that goes out from my mouth it will not return to me empty, but will accomplish what I desire and achieve the purpose for which I sent it.*

Your brother in Christ,
George Denn

November 22, 2005

<hr>

Psalms 102:18-19: *Let this be written for a future generation that a people not yet created may praise the Lord! The Lord looked down from his sanctuary on high; from heaven he viewed the earth.*

As I write this story I am sitting propped up against a tractor wheel on a sunny hillside on the far western reaches of the Ozark Mountains in Oklahoma on this beautiful fall day! Down below me is a manmade pond. Even further down below is a herd of cattle grazing undisturbed. I want to tell about three events that took place this past year back home 625 miles away. The first event happened in mid June when a tornado ripped through my place and tore off the roof of my old barn. As we have been tearing it down completely in order to rebuild, a whole lot of memories keep flooding my mind! It is funny how a simple building can influence a person's life. I remember the hayloft where we stored countless tons of hay over the years. It was a place to play as a child and a place to pray as an adult! One of the memories of the place is of my dad splicing the big hay rope on a rainy day that had broken theday before, so we could continue to fill our barn with hay! It reminds me of our Savior, Jesus Christ; although our lives can be broken, there is nothing he can't fix over time! There was the large haymow door that opened to let the block and tackle system pull the hay into the barn. I remember jumping out of this door holding an umbrella like the cartoon characters did! As I recall, this didn't work out too well, and as usual God was watching out for me or I wouldn't be able to tell about it! Of course down below is where we milked our cows and kept other animals. It is also the place where I cried out for God to help me when my ways wouldn't work anymore! I did find Him there, which is fitting, as Jesus the Son of God was born in a barn (Luke 2:7). Yes, I have many fond memories of this building, and like a relative that has passed away I will miss it! I will let its memory literally warm me this winter as I am using its wood for fuel to keep my house warm. I guess my mother was right after all; she always said I would bring the whole barn in the house if I could! It is neat, though, that a building will go back into the soil in the formof ashes on the farm that its wood came from originally, from trees that were here before most of our ancestors were!

The second event was the death of my mother; in one of my previous stories I mentioned the rare fatal disease that she had called Cortical Basil Ganglionic Degeneration. Death is an interesting part of life, and when the very person who gave you life dies, you just know your days are numbered also. Mom was at peace through all of this, because she knew the Lord and Savior, Jesus Christ, who promises eternal life for those who truly believe in his name (John 3:36). It was interesting that although Mom had a fatal disease, her death brought about the start of healing in relationships. One for me personally was a person I hadn't seen in ten and half years and we were once best friends! As I recall I was mad about a situation that had come between us that I won't discuss here, we both know what it is! So forgive me, Mike, for those hurtful words I spoke to you on that day long ago. Time really does heal old wounds. It took a lot for you and Bev to come to my mother's wake; I have to say it's probably more than I would have been able to do. Thanks again for coming, and I do look forward to resuming our friendship! Also, during the noon meal I had the opportunity to witness five people sitting around a table talking — Jerome and Julie, and Tim and Terry and Brad — which was like seeing people from three different stages of my life talking to one another! Also during the funeral I was able to tell a real funny story about something that happened long ago when my mom was extremely mad at me, and the hay barn provided a place of safety for me to run to! That was the first time I heard a church break out in laughter during a funeral! But that is the way my mom wanted people to remember her, and that is the way I will. Besides, death is really only the beginning for those who put their hope in Jesus Christ!

The third event, which was really the first event to take place this year, was when I had the opportunity to help a young man of fifteen years of age. This young man's father had killed himself when the boy was nine. I first met this young man several years ago, and with my association with the youth camps he attended I also got acquainted with his mom, who thought she had the most disruptive son at the camp! This was said of him by his mother, and I had to laugh because actually I was probably no better and in a lot of ways much worse when I was his age! For those of you who can remember me at age fifteen, I chewed tobacco, smoked, swore just about every other word, and was very boisterous (and many other things too numerous to mention)! I assured this young man's mom that if God could touch my heart, He would do the same for her son, and I committed to pray for her son on a regular basis.

Sometime after last Christmas his mom e-mailed me saying the condition of her son had grown worse and was even at times suicidal. I read this e-mail not minutes after listening to a tape on the Good Samaritan. The main point of the message was that your neighbor is anyone who is within your power to help. The Bible says sometimes these tough spirits don't come out unless we pray and fast, so I made the commitment to pray and fast for the young man. I had a sense that he was not beyond help, and I made the offer that he might come up here for a season to help me farm. An agreement was made that he would stay with me from about April 1 to sometime in November. It was always my hope that somehow the Lord would work a miracle in this young man's heart! Many people were concerned for him and joined with me in prayer and fasting for him. It wasn't long after he was here that I started to wonder what I had gotten myself into! He seemed to be forever against me and challenged my outlook on things, and he was almost always argumentative. I found myself praying daily for wisdom and knowledge as to how to deal with this guy! I came to realize there were some strong spiritual forces that were trying to destroy this young man! So I enlisted more people to pray with me and for him! His parents were praying for us unceasingly (his mom had remarried). At the same time my finances were being strained also. So it was a tough situation — here I had a fifteen-year-old under my care and a financial crisis besides, but I was darned if I was going to give up on this young man even though on many days I wanted to! As spring gave way to summer and summer gave way to fall, God did do a work in this young man's heart. Nate and I took him home on November 3 to be reunited with his family. I have more hope for him now than I've ever had, and I cried as I said good-bye. In this time of Thanksgiving I thank all those who prayed for us and helped with this young man; I truly believe God put us all together for a great purpose.

> **Psalm 102:23-28:** *In the course of my life he broke my strength he cut short my days. So I said, "Do not take me away oh my God in the midst of my days. Your years go on through all generations. In the beginning you laid the foundations of the earth, and the heavens are the work of your hands. They will perish, but you will remain. They will all wear out like a garment. Like clothing you will change them and they will be discarded, but you remain the same, and your years will never end. The children of your servants will live in your presents. Their descendants will be established before you."*

Your brother in Christ,
George Denn

February 6, 2006

⊸∞∞⊸

Isaiah 55:6-9: *Seek the Lord while he may be found; call on him while he is near. Let the wicked forsake his way and the evil man his thoughts. Let him turn to the Lord, and he will have mercy on him, and to our God he will freely pardon. "For my thoughts are not your thoughts, neither are your ways my ways," declares the Lord." As the heavens are higher than the earth, so are my ways higher than your ways and my thoughts than your thoughts.*

A couple weeks ago my neighbor John came over to my place to get a bale of hay for his horses. While we were talking he was asking me if I needed to go anywhere shortly. John is a pilot of a small airplane, and he needed to get some hours in for some training he was taking. I was telling him that I was pretty sure my friend Brad was trying to get back up here from Oklahoma! So we planned to fly down to Grove, Oklahoma on Saturday and come back Sunday morning. We planned to leave about 12:30 Saturday afternoon. Now, the Mankato Airport sits directly behind my farm. I can see the windsock and terminal and airplane hangars right out the back door of my house. It sits just on the other side and up a small knoll of what used to be my cow pasture. As a matter of fact, it is well known in my neighborhood that my cattle used to visit the airport! Especially the runways, but that's another story!

Airplanes fly over my house all the time. I can hear one right now flying over my house as I write this story. John said he would just stop over and pick me up. He lives just across the road from me to the north and a little west. We drove the two miles to the airport. John got the airplane fueled up and a tire pumped up and we were off. I was telling John as we took off that there were no cows on the runway today! We both laughed because we could remember when there would've been. As we took off in John's flying machine; I could see my farm down below, and I have to say that from the air even my place looks pretty good! As a matter of fact, everything from the air looks far different from the way it does down below. Some of the things that look so gigantic on earth look so puny from the sky, and things like towns and lakes and roads appear far closer than they do to one another when you're on the ground! As a matter of fact, you would have to look pretty close to see a human being; oh you can see his accomplishments, but in a couple of seconds even the biggest accomplishment doesn't seem all that big of deal from the sky. It really gives you a feel for how big God is and how important we humans are, and the fact that this God who created all this wants to have a relationship with us humans just really blows my mind every time I think of it all!

Hebrews 2:5-11: *It is not to angels that he has subjected the world to come, about which we are speaking. But there is a place where someone has testified: "What is man that you are mindful of him, the son of man that you care for him? You made him a little lower than the angels; you crowned him with glory and honor and put everything under his feet. "In putting everything under him, God left nothing that is not subject to him. Yet at present we do not see everything subject to him. But we see Jesus, who was made a little lower than the angels, now crowned with glory and honor because he suffered death so that by the grace of God he might taste death for everyone In bringing many sons to glory, it is fitting that God, for whom and through whom everything exists, should make the author of their salvation perfect through suffering. Both the one who makes men holy and those who are made holy are of the same family. So Jesus is not ashamed to call them brothers.*

In **Luke 12:7** Jesus himself said, *"Indeed, the very hairs of your head are all numbered."* As we traveled for four hours south John said it was the best tail wind that he ever flown in! I even got the chance to steer the plane for a little bit on the way down and back. But I really felt better when no one was steering than when I was! It really isn't the place not to know what you are doing! We talked about many things on the way down, and one of the things we talked about that I've pondered a lot in life is the question, If God loves us so much, then why does He allow evil and bad things to happen? The only answer I've ever been able to come up with for myself or for anyone else is this: Our lifetime isn't all that important to God in the broad scheme of things, but just as our time in the womb is important, so also our time here on earth is important, but when we are in eternity I don't think we will dwell on this earthly life any more than you and I dwell on our time spent in the womb. That's the only way I have ever been able to make sense of it all. John thought that was the best way he has ever heard it explained.

Well, we landed at Grove, Oklahoma. Brad and his friend Ron Porter picked us up and took us to lunch. We took in a Christian fellowship service called Accrete. We attended with Ron and his wife Holly and their friend Ben Jarvice. I have heard a lot about Ben these last three years, and I finally got to meet him. David Claggett was there as well as Brad's sister Tishra. It was good to see old friends, and Pastor West talked about many things that I have been thinking on for a while. Also Ron's church laid hands on him and his wife Holly and prayed for them, as he had decided to spend a few weeks up here in Minnesota to seek the Lord in a deeper way, which I felt was probably quite a stretch for Ron as his wife is twenty weeks pregnant! I felt that the Lord must be pretty important to Ron because I don't know many men who would do that!

We went to a Mexican village restaurant that evening and spent the night at Ron's house. As a pilot John was pretty concerned about keeping track of the weather conditions. There are some conditions he would not or couldn't fly in. In the morning John said that the weather conditions had improved overnight. After fueling the plane he brought it into the hangar so the frost that had formed on it over-night could thaw out; as it melted it had to be wiped off before we could leave. Some pictures were taken. Brad said goodbye to his girlfriend Kelly and Ron said goodbye to his wife Holly, and we took off for Minnesota. We had a little head wind on the way back, and we had to stop for fuel at the airport in Lamoni, Iowa, so all in all it took five hours to fly back home.

One thought I had on the way back home was that we cannot have a relationship with God very well without reading about this God in the Holy Bible, His inspired Word, any more than I could fly an airplane without taking lessons or learning what the instruments mean! Or any more than John could take off and just fly somewhere without checking the weather or having a map of how to get there. The results would be pretty terrible!

I know that God orchestrated this trip. John needed to get some flight hours in. Brad needed to get back to Minnesota. Ron needed some time away from home to seek the Lord about some things in his life, and I was just blessed enough to know everyone in the equation. Like the old saying, "It isn't what you know but who you know that gets you places!" Also, the Lord worked another miracle with my trip money; I only had $21 in my pocket when we left and I returned with $110. No one does that but the Lord, and you can ask the others about this if you don't believe me!

Jeremiah 33:2-3: *This is what the Lord says, he who made the earth, the Lord who formed it and established it-the Lord is his name: Call to me and I will answer you and tell you great and unsearchable things you do not know.*

Your brother in Christ,
George Denn

April 2, 2006

⸺◦⸺

Isaiah 49:23-24: *Those who hope in me will not be disap-pointed. Can plunder be taken from warriors or captives rescued from the fierce?*

A couple of weeks ago on February 16 my friend Jeff stopped in. We have been praying together for a while as my local church congregation disbanded at the end of December 2005, and at the time of this writing I really haven't been lead to seek out another congregation. So we take communion together once a week. Jeff said, "George, I've really got something crazy to ask you, and if you say yes you'll do okay and if you say no you'll do okay. I want you to write me out a check for $150,000!" No, you are not reading wrong — he actually said $150,000! At first I just laughed, because it reminded me of a time I wrote out a check to my neighbor Fred. I rent a field of hay from him, and he was tired of some of my round bales sitting there. He told me to just send him a check for whatever I felt his land was worth for that. So I sent him a check for zero dollars! But this was a lot different. As most of you know, I don't have that kind of money; $150 I can handle, but $150,000 is way out of my league! He explained that as a pastor he sees the result of greed and the consequences that people get themselves into, including the both of us when we resort to credit to buy things. Proverbs 22:7 says the rich rule over the poor and the borrower is servant to the lender. Now, it is interesting because Lord means master, the one you serve!

So in other words it is not too wise to be in debt! And I could beat that horse to death because in my family lineage that scenario goes back four generations!

He was telling me it would be nice to see what the opposite of greed looked like, and he was praying for an answer to this dilemma. I have been having some interesting things happening in the money department of my life lately, and my checkbook seems to be forever on the short side. Like the old song goes, there's too much month at the end of the money! He said he prayed a lot about this and the Lord led him to me. My answer was that I needed to pray about this and that I would let him know on Monday, but when Monday came I had no answer either way from the Lord. So I told Jeff maybe we both need to pray about this for ten days. So for ten days we both asked God for His answer to all of this, because if this was indeed from God I didn't want to say no! I was thinking that if GOD was going to work in this way it would be a modern-day example of the story of the widow of Zarephath found in 1 Kings 17:7-16, or the story of the widow's oil in 2 Kings 4:1-7. For ten days my mind wavered back and forth wondering what to do. So the second day of March came, D-day for my decision. I felt totally at peace about doing this, and the fact that I had peace told me this was something I should do.

Luke 1:78-79: *Because of the tender mercy of our God, by which the rising sun will come to us from heaven to shine on those living in darkness and in the shadow of death, to guide our feet into the path of peace.*

Also, Galatians 5:22 mentions peace as part of the fruit of the Holy Spirit, and 1 Corinthians 14:33 says for God is not a God of disorder but of peace. So I reckoned if I had peace about all of this it was the way to go, because God seems to be the only one who can give you peace. I also was looking for a possible miracle! In a footnote in my Bible at 1 Corinthians 12:10 it says in Scripture a miracle is an action that cannot be explained by natural means. It is an act of God intended as evidence of His power and purpose. Boy, could my finances use one of those! We drove to Kasson, Minnesota that morning where a spiritual revival was starting in that town, and we took in a seminar at the Church of Christ there. Rick Heeran was there talking about a town near the twin cites area in Elk River, Minnesota where God seems to be just totally taking the town over! In the video we watched there was a banker testifying that about 102 people had actually given their lives to the Lord and accepted Jesus Christ as their Lord and Savior inside his bank! This had also been taking place in schools, motorcycle dealerships, and car dealerships. Needless to say, this is a miracle, and it is happening to an entire town about 100 miles from me! I was thinking, *if that sort of thing can happen there, it can happen in Mankato*! For those interested in checking out their web site, it is http://www.harvestevan.org/

Well, as Jeff and I drove home from there, first I had him anoint me for "marketplace ministry," as at this time he is the closest thing to a minister that I have, and I wrote out the check for $150,000! I have to admit I was slightly nervous but nonetheless felt completely at peace about it, and based on all the indications I was receiving from the Lord, this was something I needed to do. Well, we waited and prayed about this check, and on Tuesday the 7th of March, Bernie, the president of my bank called me and left messages on both my answering machines! He said for me to call him at my earliest convenience. Jeff came over shortly after that and I told him how my banker wanted me to call him! I felt that this might be another opportunity to be a witness for the LORD and tell Bernie the story behind why we did this. Jeff said he wasn't sure that he wanted to go along with me, because his wife Peggy had found out that they suddenly had $150,000 in their bank account. By the time Jeff got done explaining the situation to Peggy, let's just say she wasn't all that understanding about the situation! I said, "Look, Jeff, this was your idea, and I figured Bernie deserved at least an explanation." Jeff didn't know it, but if he hadn't gone with me I possibly would have killed him and our friendship would be over! Well, maybe not killed him ... I called Bernie and he said, "George, did you write out a check for $150,000?" I said, "Yes I did!" Bernie described how it had really caught his attention, and I replied that I suppose it did! Then I went on to explain to Bernie, "But there was a story behind that check, and the guy I wrote it out to is standing right here, and we would like to come in and tell you the story."

Bernie said that would be great and that at 9 o'clock the next morning would work for him. He also mentioned that he sent the check back because the bank wouldn't cover that amount, and I said that was fine and that I was glad the bank hadn't covered it! You see, we had been praying that if someone with that kind of money came forward and just gave it to me, then that would have been a miracle. But God never seems to work the way we think He ought to! Anyway, we prayed again about our circumstances and asked God to send His angels and His Spirit to the bank to prepare Bernie for what we had to tell him; we really didn't know what we were going to say, but in all of this I was never nervous. I know that in itself was from God given the circumstances! We prayed for wisdom, and God gave me three things to give to Bernie: a copy of the book I am writing, a DVD that my church denomination had put out, "Called To Be Free," so Bernie could understand some of my Christian background, and a DVD from the harvest evangelism group by Ed Silvoso that goes into full detail about the movement of God not only in Elk River, Minnesota but also in the state of Hawaii, the prison systems in Argentina, and the difference one man made in the country of Africa! I had to go to pick up the DVD from my friend David to whom I had lent it.

There was a thick fog on that morning as we drove to the bank, and we could barely see where we were going. Once in a while a car's headlights could be seen through the fog. It seemed as if God was telling me that this fog was like the spiritual condition of the people on the earth, and once in a while you can see the glimmer of light within them, but the fog won't lift until the sun shines, so neither will the spiritual fog lift until Jesus the Son shines in their life.

Psalm 4-6: *Many are asking, "Who can show us any good"? Let the light of your face shine upon us, O Lord.*

When we pulled into the bank parking lot, we knew that God had gone before us, because on the bank sign it said, "You have to stand for something or you will fall for anything!" We met with Bernie and had a real good conversation. To explain the story behind the $150,000 check, Jeff shared his thoughts on how he wouldn't mind seeing what the opposite of greed would look like in this part of the world, and that it had been our intention to have fun trying to do that! Bernie said that he has seen a lot of the effects of greed on his side of the spectrum. I mentioned to Bernie that he had indeed been out to my place some fifteen years back when the bank first opened; Bernie and his boss had stopped out to visit us; being a new bank in town, they were looking for business. I clearly remembered that day: Dad and I were putting some hay into the barn at that time, and I remember being impressed with the bankers' personal visit! So when it came time for me to choose a different bank, Bernie's bank was the one I went to.

At the end of our talk with Bernie, he seemed very receptive to our message. Before we left him, we prayed peace and blessings over Bernie and the bank and for all the people that would walk through the door of the bank! Bernie prayed for us also, so our peace was returned to us! I end today's writing on March 8, 2006. I can't see how the story ends because it hasn't finished yet! At this time there is still $150,000 in Jeff's checking account that has not been made available, so I guess I'll have to wait for another day to finish my story! **Psalm 9:1** says, *I will praise you O Lord, with all my heart; I will tell of all your wonders.*

Well, it is now the 20th of March; it has been a little more than a month since I got involved in this story, so I thought I'd better write this down, because things aren't over yet! On the weekend of March 10-12 I was up at my friend Gordy's; he lives about forty miles west of Duluth, Minnesota, and he has a lake in front of his house, so I went up for a weekend of fishing. While I was there I was telling Gordy this story. He was amazed to say the least, and then he said, "You know, it will be interesting to see Jeff's response if the check doesn't clear the bank." Then we found out on Sunday that the check hadn't cleared, so we pretty much thought that was the end of our story. However, like the story in Ezekiel chapter 37 about the valley of the dry bones, The Lord breathed life into this story. On Saturday evening there was a number on my cell phone from someone who had tried to call me. I returned the call and a man answered, "This is the House of Hope in Mankato, Minnesota!" This man said he didn't know who had tried to call me, but he said he would put it on the bulletin board that George had called them back. On Monday I found out from Jeff that his bank had sent my check back to my bank again. I was thinking, *great, if God doesn't make the check good I'll get charged another $25.* Then I started wondering about that call from the House of Hope. Now, I don't know anyone there, but I do know that God talks a lot about hope in the Bible, so therefore God is a house of hope! Psalm 25:3 says that no one whose hope is in God will ever be put to shame, but that they will be put to shame who are treacherous without excuse. Well every day we prayed together about this situation with the check. I had to leave for Illinois on Friday and didn't return until today at noon. I went to pick up my mail and meet Jeff for prayer and communion. When he showed me his bank statement dated the 3rd of March, it showed that the funds were available for his use — $150,000! So we prayed about this and decided to wait a few more days to see what would happen.

Psalm 42:5-6: *Why are you so downcast, O my soul? Why are you so disturbed within me? Put your hope in God, for I will yet praise him my Savior and my God.*

Well, it is now March 22. Yesterday and today have been very interesting days to say the least! Yesterday I called Bernie at the bank to see if he could give me any information as to why now there were $150,000 available to draw from in my friend Jeff's account. Bernie told me that he had no idea, as he said he hadn't seen the check since he had sent it back to Jeff's bank on the 7th of March.

That answered my question — this didn't take place within my bank! So I called my friend Jeff and said, "Now the ball's in your court," so he said he would call his bank in the morning. So this morning Jeff came by at 7 am to pray about all of this. I was a little tired; I had gotten up at around 3:00 this morning because I couldn't sleep from thinking about all of this, so I read a little in the Bible and went back to sleep at 5:00 a.m. So I was pretty tired when Jeff came over at 7 am. After we prayed about the situation with the check, Jeff went home and I went out to haul some hay.

Proverbs 10:22: *The blessing of the Lord brings wealth, and adds no trouble to it.*

About 11:00 am I came back into the house, and on my phone answering system was a message from Nick, who is the president of Jeff's bank. He said to call him back as soon as possible, as it was very urgent! *Hmm, I wonder what that is about!* So I called Jeff to tell him this information, and he said this was interesting, because he had called his bank and wanted to talk to a lady whose name is Sharon, and she hadn't gotten back to him yet! He also said that almost immediately after he got off the phone with his bank that the funds for the $150,000 were pulled from the available status and once again put on the unavailable status! Very interesting! Then when Jeff and I had lunch today and we were talking about this and wondering how something so simple could become so complicated! I told him how I've had people give me checks before that had bounced and eventually I get the check back. We prayed for wisdom on my part as to what to say to Nick, and after we finished praying I called him.

Nick wondered if I really had written a check for $150,000 to Jeff, and I said that yes I had, and he was wondering if this wasn't something that I needed to discuss with Jeff. I told Nick that Jeff was my best friend and that we had already been discussing this check since February! Nick was wondering if this situation was something that was going to affect our friendship in any way. I assured him that it wouldn't; I mean really, what is $150,000 anyway between friends? Nick felt that this was all "very strange." Nick wanted to know if I had changed my mind and wanted to stop this process, because if he sent the check back to my bank it would cost me another $25 if I didn't have enough funds to cover it, and Jeff would be charged another $5. I told him to send the check back to my bank because neither Jeff nor I wanted to be the ones to put a stop to this process. (If indeed this was from the Lord, we didn't want to be the ones to stop it!)

Nick was telling me that if the federal authorities were to conduct an investigation about this whole thing, they may press charges, but then in the same breath he also said that in this case that probably wouldn't be applicable! I told Nick there was a story behind the check if he wanted to hear it, but he said that wouldn't be necessary, but that if this was some sort of game between us it needed to stop. I assured him that it was no game and that Jeff and I took all of this very seriously! Once again, if this was from God, there was no way we wanted to be the ones to stop it regardless of the check charges, because it still allows God to perform a miracle if He so chooses.

About an hour and a half later after I'd talked to Nick on the phone, Jeff called and he said, "Well George, the plot thickens." Sharon had just called him back and said that the check had been sent to the Federal Reserve on Monday the 13th of March, and that they had called my bank on that day and someone from my bank had said that the funds would be there! So they sent the check to the Federal Reserve, but the Federal Reserve doesn't keep checks like that so they should have sent the check back to my bank, but nobody anywhere seems to know the whereabouts of this check! So now Sharon was going to call my bank to see if she could find out who it was who had said that the check would be good. So now two and a half hours have lapsed, and Jeff hasn't heard back from Sharon, but her boss Nick seems to have some information about it. So we have two somewhat different stories coming from the same bank.

Proverbs 9:10: *The fear of the Lord is the beginning of wisdom, and knowledge of the Holy One is understanding.*

March 23, 2006: As I write down some thoughts about this story, there are several interesting things that cannot be explained at this time.

I remembered how Peggy had told us that she'd heard there had been another person in the car with Jeff when he had cashed the check! When Peggy called the bank to inquire about $150,000 the drive-up teller said she had seen someone else in the car with him, but Jeff said there was no one else in the car with him that day! *Hmmm ...*

Next, the House of Hope calling me while I was up at Gordy's for the weekend of the March 12th, but nobody there knew what I was talking about!

Next,the person at my bank who said that the funds would be available, but now no one seems to know who that mysterious person was!

Next, the funds being available for three days, but then once again were placed on the unavailable list ... and, Jeff had said that they always show the history of his account on his receipts, but suddenly today they didn't show them!

Next, the two conflicting stories at Jeff's bank between Nick and Sharon, and no one seems to know for sure where the check is!

And last night I found out that this Sharon just happens to be a neighbor to my sister Marie!

Well, we just have to see what plays out today. I am reminded of Job 42:1-2 where Job replied to the Lord, "I know that you can do all things, no plan of yours can be thwarted." Later this afternoon Sharon called me and left a message that I should call her. I called Jeff to see if Sharon had tried to call him. He said he was ten minutes from his home and that he would call me back after he got home and had a chance to check his messages. About ten minutes later he called me back and said that yes, she had tried to call him. Jeff and I have come to see that through this whole thing we've needed to pray for wisdom as to what to say and what to do, because we had no idea what God was up to in all of this! So we prayed on the phone, and then he called Sharon; she told him that the check was in Mapleton, Minnesota and it was heading back to my bank, and at this point they were sure that the check would bounce. Once again neither Jeff nor I wanted to stop this process that the Lord had led us to in the first place, and we still feel that there is room for God to work a miracle if He so chooses, because it is His glory we seek and not ours! We followed what His Spirit told us to do, and He had led us to this point.

Isaiah 3:10-11: *Tell the righteous it will be well with them, for they will enjoy the fruit of their deeds. Woe to the wicked! for disaster is upon them! They will be paid back for what their hands have done.*

Proverbs 3:5-6: *Trust in the Lord with all your heart and lean not on your own understanding; in all of your ways acknowledge him and he will make your paths straight.*

Well, here it is April 2ⁿᵈ; its been five weeks now since that check was cashed, and the folks at Jeff's bank were positive we would get that check back sometime last week! However, neither of us has heard a thing about it — no check returns, no phone calls, no cops coming to pick me up, nothing!

As I end this story I'll let you wonder along with me what might continue to unfold, just as I have had to wonder these many weeks.

In **Matthew 18:19-20** Jesus himself said, *"Again, I tell you that if two of on earth agree about anything you ask for, it will be done for you by my Father in heaven. For where two or three come together gathered in my name, there am I with them."*

Well, it has been our prayer throughout this whole process that this check would accomplish everything that God wanted it to! I can tell you some things that it has accomplished. It has healed a friendship that wasn't the best for the last couple of years. It has brought to my attention the Harvest Ministries, which I have been putting into practice in my own life and introducing to all of my friends, and it isn't costing them a dime In training materials. I also got to have a chat with the president of my bank. All these things that I can see and all the things I cannot see would not have happened if I hadn't written out that check for $150,000.

At the end of this interesting story, I have to say to you anyone reading this book; please do not try to duplicate this, as this is something the Lord led us to do in being obedient to the Holy Spirit. God probably has something far different for you to do! All I will suggest is that you try being obedient to what God wants you to do; you might find it goes against what common sense is telling you!

Matthew 14:27-29: *But Jesus immediately said to them "take courage it is I. Don't be afraid." Lord if it is you," Peter replied," tell me to come to you on the water." "Come," he* *said. Then Peter got down out of the boat, walked on the water and came toward Jesus.*

Peace and Blessings to you all!
Your friend in Christ,\ George Denn

May 13, 2006

⚭

Romans 4:-17: *Therefore the promise comes by faith, so that it may be by grace and may be guaranteed to all Abraham's offspring — not only to those who are of the law but to those who are of the faith of Abraham. He is the father of us all. As it is written, "I have made you a father of many nations." He is our father in the sight of God, in whom he believed — the God who gives life to the dead and calls things that are not as though they were.*

I have been cooped up in my house this cold, rainy May day, except for one person coming to buy some wheat from me and my neighbor David stopping for a cup of coffee and a chat. I call him one of my coffee buzzards! And then my friend Steve took me to lunch. I have had one of those do-nothing days. Just about the time I figured I would probably never write anything again and I would probably just die from boredom and despair, I was looking out my kitchen window when I saw a beautiful rainbow, a reminder of God's covenant to Noah that never again would He destroy the entire earth with water (Genesis 9:12-13). That covenant extends to us in the present day as well. After seeing that rainbow, I was inspired to write this. After publishing as an article the last story written here, I received a whirlwind of comments —some were concerned for me, some were wondering about me. I am reminded of something my dear departed mother said to me on more than one occasion: "What's the matter with you? Do you need your head examined?" I guess I have to admit there are days when I wonder about that myself! I thought I'd better explain some of the events leading up to the check-writing episode and maybe share some of the comments received afterward.

I would have to say that 80 percent of the people who commented said it was an interesting story. You are people after my own heart! For those other 20 percent, I appreciate your concern, but I would challenge you to lighten up a bit as you only go through this life once. My favorite saying about money comes from the movie "Hello, Dolly" — Money is like manure it is no good unless you spread it around! As a farmer I can understand that completely! The first event that led up to my last story happened on October 18, 2005 around nine o'clock in the morning. I was coming home with a load of hay from another farm and Ky was following me in my little pickup, when all of a sudden in the opposite lane coming in my direction, for no reason and without slowing down, a tandem gravel truck careened off the road, jumped a field driveway, and drove the nose of that truck into the embankment of the ditch! The impact busted the front tires off, and gravel flew fifty feet over the front of the cab of the dump truck! The trucker's head hit the windshield, and the windshield popped out and little pieces of glass went flying everywhere! I was the first guy on the scene, and I figured the man was dead as he was just twitching in the driver's seat. I could get to him easily because his door had been torn off as well. But to my surprise this giant of a man came to and got out of the truck cab, but he was really shaken up. I told him to just sit down on the grass till we could get some help! He wanted to use my cell phone to call his boss to tell him of the accident. By that time another man had shown up to see what he could do to help, and I figured we ought to call 911 first. This other fellow said, "I'll call for help on my phone," so I let the trucker call his boss on mine. I told Ky to go ahead on home, especially because he seemed really shocked from having witnessed this accident! I noticed a slogan on the side of the truck that read, "Bury the past or dig for the future!" I can remember thinking, *Okay, God, You have my attention!* If that truck had turned the other way, he would have plowed into Ky and me both, and we would have been flatter than two pancakes! Considering that the driver could've only turned left or right, I figure it's a 50 percent chance that I'm writing this now!

The next major event leading up to the check-writing incident happened on November 12, 13, and 14, 2005. Brad and I had planned to go visit some friends for the weekend up in Duluth. Everything imaginable went on that Friday morning to delay us, and we just couldn't seem to get going for nothing, and when we finally did get going we were extremely late! The plan was to go to a fish fry in Duluth that evening and then go to a Ken Davis show after that. My friend said that if we went to the fish fry we would be too late for the show, so we decided to eat fast food at Wendy's instead. After we had sat down to eat, I looked up, and a couple of tables over sat someone who looked just like my dad's cousin Joanne! My table was chanting "George Denn, George Denn" trying to get her attention; I was embarrassed because I wasn't totally sure it was her, but it was! I was four hours from my home and she was two hours from her home, and when I went over to talk to her, my phone rang and it was my Dad; needless to say this amazed everyone at my table!

The next day as we were going home from church my friend said, "George, what's the story on your pickup?" I told him it was in the shop, and that they wanted $3001 to pay for repairs before I could get it back. He asked me, "What are you going to do?" I said, "I don't know; I guess I'm trusting the Lord for that answer ... what else can I do?" That afternoon he was playing some CDs, and the lyrics of one of the songs kept repeating "God will make a way where there seems to be no way." I had to laugh, because I had heard that song about a hundred times in the last ten days, it seemed like. The next song he played was "It Is Well With My Soul." I was half asleep in my chair when the music ended, and I said, "You know, it is well with my soul; I feel closer to God right now than ever before! My friend said, "Good, let's pray." After we prayed he said, "George, I have just been convicted by the Holy Spirit that I am to help you out in some way. I can't give you $3000, but I will give you half that amount on faith that someone else will come forward with the other half." And then he promptly wrote out a check that I never asked him for!

I was practically dumbfounded by this gesture, and I remembered when I left home for this trip thinking that I wouldn't be able to earn any money while being away this weekend! I had also told Brad before we left that I sure could use a couple new caps to wear, as mine were getting mighty tacky. On Sunday, and without any prior knowledge, my friend was digging around in a closet as he said, "George, could you use a couple new hats?" Well, on the way home my mind was wavering about that $1500 check; should I use the money to pay towards my pickup or should I pay on some rent I still owe? I chose the rent, and for the next couple of weeks absolutely no money came in! I rode to Oklahoma with Brad for Thanksgiving, and when I got back Brad and I had been hauling some firewood when I almost wiped out on a snowy road in my old Ford. I said, "That's it, let's go get my other pickup out of the shop!" Brad kept telling me, "You only have $800 and it will cost $3000!" I said, "Well, that's close enough!" He said, "You're really going to do it, aren't you?!" I told him that I fully believed God would supply my need, and I sure would enjoy having my Dodge back because at least it has good brakes! Also that evening I was using the old Ford to take some hay bales to the end of my drive to throw on an old truck I use for selling hay, and when I drove alongside that truck a hook grabbed the mirror and tore it off, which then bent the door, so I got my Dodge home just in time! As I lay in bed that night I was wondering if I should have done that! I still owed them $2200, and that was a lot to be short! All of a sudden this feeling of joy started bubbling up from within me — I don't know how else to explain it! The next day before I was even out of bed yet the phone started ringing, which continued practically nonstop all day. It seemed everyone needed hay or wood on that day! At 3 o'clock that afternoon I told Brad that I had $1200 and that I was only $1000 short now! Brad was saying, "Man, George, you put yourself in positions where you make God do things." I told Brad that God didn't have to do anything if He didn't want to! Before I went to the bank I stopped at the mailbox to get the mail, and there was a government farm program check in there for $1100! All I could say at the time was praise the Lord!

Hebrews 11:1: Now faith is the **substance** of things hoped for, the **evidence** of things **not seen** (NKJV).

The next event happened on January 8, 2006, when my Dad and I and his cousins Delma and Donna were at Donna's daughter Nancy's house about five miles east of Momence, Illinois. We were all sitting around the table talking about Jesus, and Delma made the comment that she could just feel His presence! I was explaining to Nancy my theory of how the disciple Peter could walk on water because he wasn't subject to the law of gravity at that time. I base this on Galatians chapters 3 and 4 and a Bible study Dan Rogers gave about six years ago that the meaning of the word "law" here means "any law under the cosmos." Suddenly Nancy exclaimed, "How in the h—- is this coffee pot making coffee?! The filter and the coffee are not in the coffeemaker!" Everyone just sat around looking dumbfounded when I said, "That is the sort of thing I am talking about!"

We were all visiting Nancy again on April 30th, and she said, "You know, George, I could feel your presence for days after you left!" I assured her that it wasn't my presence she had felt but instead it was the Holy Spirit's presence! Interestingly enough, the day of the coffeepot miracle was the first time I had seen Nancy in about thirty-five years. And Delma and Donna are sisters to Joanne, my dad's cousin that I ran into at Wendy's that night in Duluth! I told this story to my friend Jeff, and later he mentioned to me that he had told that story to his prayer group, and somebody there mentioned that if Jesus could turn water into wine, he imagined He could make coffee as well!

About a week later Jeff stopped in and said, "George, I had an experience like your coffee story!" Jeff said that he had a gift card to Baker's Square that someone had given to him for Christmas, and even though he had used it only once, and he was certain beyond a shadow of a doubt that there was less than $1 remaining on it, after services he took his family out to eat and thought he would use up that last $1 on the card and write a check for the remainder of the bill, but to his surprise the card paid for the meal! With all these little miracles Jeff felt that God was trying to say something to us that we weren't comprehending, which led him into prayer for three weeks, which eventually led him to ask me to write that check.

On a different note, I thought it would be fun to share some of the comments I received after writing the article about the check-writing episode!

One person said the story perplexed him. This man who used to work for me long ago!

A pastor and a chef gave me some phony million-dollar bills saying maybe they would help us out!

One person thought Jeff was sent from Satan and was trying to lead me astray. I thought that too once upon a time, but I was in a totally different mindset than I am now.

One guy who's a landscaper said, "Something good is going to happen as a result!"

My cousin Peter is an accountant, and he said, "You're d**m lucky you're not in jail!" But then, maybe that is the miracle, because I believe there is no such thing as luck!

One person told me he thought I had provoked the Holy Spirit in a good way. And it wouldn't surprise him if $150,000 would miraculously appear this man spent 20 years working with troubled youth and has a degree in psychology!

One pastor said, "I can see you writing out a check for $150,000, George, but it surprises me about Jeff."

One person said he thought it would be cool if a miracle like that would happen, but his wife thought we were testing God.

My favorite one is this one though, which came from a pastor: He said he didn't know about a coffee pot making coffee without the coffee in it.

I find this interesting! A coffee pot holds 10-12 cups and the six stone jars in John 2 hold 20-30 gallons apiece; wine is purple and coffee is brown, and both are a common drink of their day. Also I sat around a table with this person some time ago listening to people tell story after story about miracles! For instance one woman was telling how; she drove to town and back in a rainstorm in a car with no windshield wipers because her husband had taken them off to replace them, and as she drove to town and back it rained all around her car but never on it! Another woman was in a tent at a worship service when a tornado was heading right for the tent. Everyone inside was praying for God to protect them, and the tornado split and went around them!

And then, this pastor told of a time when he was driving a car and another car was approaching the intersection in the lane perpendicular to his; both cars were going full speed ahead and that car should have broadsided him, but as the impact occurred, that car miraculously bounced and spun around several times, and neither car ever crashed and neither car ever stopped! And he said, "Boy, you could write a whole story on the miracles that have happened to people sitting around this table", but yet he doesn't know about a coffee pot making coffee without grounds or a filter. I am sorry but I find that way too humorous! But as long as there is time and human beings on earth we will probably look at things differently! I could go on and on and on telling stories of the responses to my last story.

Here is something for us all! **Romans 4:21-25:** *Being fully persuaded that God had power to do what he had promised. This is why "it was credited to him as righteousness." The words "it was credited to him" were written not for him alone, but also for us to whom God will credit righteousness — for us who believe in him who raised Jesus our Lord from the dead. He was delivered over to death for our sins and was raised to life for our justification.*

Now that I look back on all that I've written in this entry, I guess God did make something out of this dreary day after all. Peace and blessings to you!

Your brother in Christ,
George Denn

June 5, 2006

⚬⚬⚬

Matthew 25:1-4: *"At that time the kingdom of heaven will be like ten virgins who took their lamps and went out to meet the bridegroom. Five of them were foolish and five were wise. The foolish ones took their lamps but did not take any oil with them. The wise, however, took oil in jars along with their lamps."*

My neighbor David likes to call me most mornings around 6 am trying to catch me early in the day before I get busy with farm duties, but today I was already driving down the road when he called. He was telling me that he had really done a stupid thing; he had forgotten to put crop oil in the mixture of his chemicals to control weeds in his corn. Crop oil helps the chemicals to work! He might have to re-spray all his corn, which could end up being very costly. Just like in the scripture from Matthew quoted here where the five foolish virgins forgot to bring oil for their lamps and it really ended up costing them! This refers to the Holy Spirit, and at this time of year that I find myself running in four directions all at once — hay to put up, pumpkins to weed, graduations to attend, and taking care of the older folks in my life. Sometimes I get so busy that I find it very easy not to listen to God and what He wants me to do for his kingdom. Not wanting to forget my oil, I am prompted to write this story.About two weeks ago, my friend Tom Kennebeck from Orr, Minnesota called me saying, "George, when you come to church on Sunday, could you give a brief talk on walking in the Spirit?" I told Tom I would be paying attention to things and maybe have a story to tell! I had a graduation to go to up that way and a day of fishing with a few friends planned; also, Jeff wanted to go fishing for a few days. By Tuesday, though, I could tell this wasn't going to be your ordinary fishing trip with all the things that started "going wrong" — lack of finances, insurance salesman coming to collect payment a month too soon, and my weed trimmer throwing a stone through the back window of my pickup! By Thursday I was worse than penniless. Several of us had decided to go to the Marketplace Ministry luncheon held in Mankato. Lunch was $10, and I was under the assumption that our tickets had been paid for. I was wrong! I was wondering how I was going to pull this one off when Jeff asked if he could buy my lunch? I said sure! I was thinking, *how can I go on this fishing trip when I can't even buy lunch my own lunch?*

Chuck Ripka was our speaker. Chuck was telling us how God had been using him in the marketplace. Chuck is a banker from Elk River. One of the interesting things he was telling us was how God asked him to resign his position as senior vice president of Riverview Bank in Otsego, Minnesota, and start an international bank, and how God instructed him to give 51 percent of the profits back to the glory of God. The Lord told him if he would listen to him he would never have to worry about the bottom line again! Chuck was telling us that he hasn't even got the computers running yet and different countries have been calling him to start banks in their countries. I was thinking it would be neat to be able to talk to this guy but that I probably wouldn't get the chance. We were just about ready to leave when Jeff said, "I have to ask that guy a question!" So I did get to meet and talk to Chuck briefly. (Chuck holds seminars every so often in Elk River. He calls his business Rivers International, and you can contact Chuck about his seminars by email at cjripka@aol.com or phone 612-812-4248 for prayer and all your international banking needs.)

After the luncheon I was still getting ready to go fishing even though it seemed impossible. Then I went to get my mail and there was a $500 check for some work that I had done for someone! We left for Orr on Friday at 12:22 in the afternoon and arrived exactly six hours later. We camped out at Tom Burnett's cabin on the west side of Pelican Lake, but we did get to hang out at Tom and Jenny's place one evening. Tom and his brother Jake played guitars and Jeff played his violin. On Sunday we had the opportunity to attend Tom Kennebeck's church. We also introduced to Tom the idea of Marketplace Ministry and prayed with Tom for the city of Orr. I hope someday Tom and Chuck Ripka can meet one another! On Tuesday we got to fish with Gordy and his friend Moose and Moose's grandson T. Tom K. took us out on the company pontoon boat. That thing even had reclining seats — now that's what I call fishing! That evening a guy by the name of Glenn joined us, so we had a great day of brotherhood!

I saw one of the most interesting insects while we were there; these water bugs would come up out of the water and sit on a blade of grass, and then suddenly a dragonfly would burst out of this bug, dry off, and leave the discarded shell of his former life behind! How amazing is that! That's a good analogy of what it will be like when we get our spirit bodies and how different they will be from these earthly bodies.

1 Corinthians 15:42-44: *So it will be with the resurrection of the dead. The body that was sown is perishable, it is raised imperishable it is sown in dishonor it is raised in glory; it is sown in weakness, it is raised in power; it is sown a natural body, it is raised a spiritual body. If there is a natural body, there is also a spiritual body.*

Well, the dragonflies took off after the mosquitoes that were pestering us, so thank God for small miracles! There also was a hailstorm that was unlike any I have ever seen. For ten minutes golf ball-sized hail slowly plunked from the sky. It was an awesome site to see the big splashes on the lake as we watched from inside the cabin. Also, we caught lots of fish; my biggest one was a 21-inch bass, but it was full of eggs so I let it go. The best bait all week was just a humble plain hook and a night crawler and I have a new name for Canadian geese. Gordy's friend Moose calls them Sky Carp! So I'll never look at these geese in the same old way as before.

Another incident made me think. Jeff and I were fishing by this island. We were close to shore, and there were a lot of rocks underneath us; when it was time to pull up the anchor, it wouldn't budge. We figured it must be wedged between two rocks, so Jeff jumped in the lake and try to get the anchor loose. I was reminded of these song lyrics: "Be very sure your anchor holds and grips the solid rock". We ended up having to cut the anchor rope after all was said and done! But speaking of the sureness of anchors, I figure if you are kept by Jesus Christ, then there is no higher power that you can be protected by.

Jude 1:1: *To those who have been called, who are loved by God the Father and kept by Jesus Christ.*

I'll end this fishing story with another fishing story. **John 21:5-6** says, He called out to them, "Friends, haven't you any fish?" "No," they answered. He said, "Throw your net on the right side of the boat and you will find some." When they did, they were unable to haul the net in because of the large number of fish.

My question to you is, what side of the boat is your net on? Peace and blessings to you!

Your brother in Christ,
George Denn

July 5, 2006

———∞∞∞———

Philippians 2:1-5: *If you have any encouragement from being with Christ, if any comfort from his love, if any fellowship with the Spirit, if any tenderness and compassion, than make my joy complete by being like minded, having the same love, being one in spirit and purpose. Do nothing out of selfish ambition or vain conceit, but in humility consider others better than yourselves. Each of you should look not only to your own interests, but also to the interests of others. Your attitude should be the same as that of Christ Jesus.*

I have to admit most days I fall real short of that mark! That was a section of scripture that was used as the theme for the five day canoe trip eleven of us went on in the boundary waters called The Servants Passage. Actually, we used all of verses 1-18. For three weeks after I returned from my last adventure I was just buried in work! I had 165 acres of hay to put up and 30 acres of pumpkins to spray one row at a time with my riding lawn mower, which took me about a good five days just to spray the pumpkins! I had some late soybeans to plant and to spray before I went on this trip. I wasn't sure I would be going on this trip, as I absolutely needed to get this all done before I went. So I left the decision up to God. I said to myself, If I get done, God wants me to go, and if I don't get done, then God doesn't want me to go! Also, I need some money to take along, and that wasn't looking too promising either for three weeks leading up to our departure date. One of the stipulations for this two-year course I've been taking is that I'm supposed to have a mentor. So I called

Pastor Doug Johannsen to see if he would be interested in being my mentor. He said he would but that he really didn't know how to mentor anyone. I told him that was OK, as I didn't know how to be mentored. So we both agreed this could be interesting! I needed to be done with my work on the 24th of June; actually the 23rd would be even better, because I wanted to attend Jim and Melody Hime's wedding. I finished my work at 9:00 pm on the 23rd, went to the wedding on the 24th, and left for Orr at 8:30 Sunday morning on the 25th. My finances were still an issue. Can a person travel six hours one way and back on $46? Sure you can! I had some gas in the tank, so I put 60 gallons in my portable fuel tank and put that in back of my pickup; filled my pickup with gas and I was out of here! On the way I stopped at an outdoor church service/picnic in the Twin Cities, and from there a friend of mine named Dan Jensen rode with me the rest of the way. One peculiar thing that happened on this trip was I made it all the way up to Orr on one tank of gas; I have never come close to that before. So I figured I had some divine help! Eleven of us took part in this adventure: Doug and Betty, big James and little James, Tammy, Kay, Lois, Robert, Dan, Tom and me.

We started at Crane Lake and paddled a couple hours before we stopped for a break. One of the first things I noticed as I steered our canoe was that it was leaking! I yelled out to the rest of the crew that we were leaking, but they thought it was just from our clothes dripping! As the water got deeper in the canoe, we found out that my theory was the correct one! When we stopped for a break, we bailed ten gallons of water from the canoe. Tom fixed the leak later with a piece of gum and some duct tape! Anyway, we had to pull off the lake because it was time for lunch and it was starting to rain. We all took shelter under our ponchos or a tarp. I figured it was a good time for a nap. When the rain let up some Tom jokingly said, "George can build us a fire!" Some were sort of teasing me because I had brought along my big ax, but little did they know I had brought some diesel fuel along that I had in a dish soap bottle hid in my tackle box, and in no time we had a nice fire going! So because of all that and the ability to swing an ax, I received the nickname of Paul Bunyan — what can I say?! We stopped at an island and stayed there for two days because of rain, but the fishing was good, and we saw one of the most impressive double rainbows, and the reflection of a sunset in the water almost made it look like a double sunset.

We had come on this trip to seek God and to discover how He was revealing Himself to us. I was particularly interested in that part as it seemed God had been giving me the silent treatment for some time now! I found a rock with a cleft in it. As I was sitting there I thought of the verse of the hymn called "He Hideth My Soul":

A wonderful Savior is Jesus my Lord,A wonderful Savior to me;He hideth my soul in the cleft of the rock,Where rivers of pleasure I see.

He hideth my soul in the cleft of the rock,
That shadows a dry, thirsty land;
He hideth my life in the depths of His love,
And covers me there with His hand,
And covers me there with His hand.

I was also thinking how our perfection is found in Jesus Christ. **Hebrews 10:14** says, *because by one sacrifice he has made perfect forever those who are being made holy.* Later I was fishing on this spot when four people drove by in a boat, and when one of the women saw the perfect spot I had found she called out, "now there is perfection!" That statement really confirmed my earlier thoughts. Another time I was walking on the beach wondering what God was up to in my life, and at that moment I looked down and saw a button that had the words I AM etched on it! I thought that was interesting, because that is one of the names God uses to describe Himself! In **Exodus 3 14** *God said to Moses, "I AM who I AM. This is what you are to say to the Israelites. 'I AM has sent me to you.'"*

So I was happy as it seemed that now God was talking to me again. As I was swimming/bathing I looked across the lake, which was as smooth as glass, and I saw God's abundance all around me. It all looked so huge, and I felt so very small. I just thanked God for it all at that moment in time. On the morning when we left, I got the impression that this place for some reason seemed too perfect to be real; I don't know how else to describe it. Before we left I made a point to leave enough wood so that others who came along after us would have enough to build a fire without having to go look for it. The very next island we camped at someone had left a whole pile of wood that had been sawed with a chainsaw, and all we had to do was split it up. There was way more wood than we could use! I was reminded of this scripture:

> **Luke 6:38:** *Give and it will be given to you a good measure, pressed down, shaken together and running over will be poured into your lap. For the same measure you use, it will be measured to you.*

Not too far from where we camped, Doug and Dan took Tammy to show her the spot where her son Josh had been baptized a year earlier! Tammy was filled with emotion at being able to visit this spot. Tom, big James, and Kay seemed to have some connections with two other parties that were camped nearby. What was interesting was how they just walked up to us and just started talking to them! We all felt that it was a moment in time that God was doing a work in their lives.

On the last stretch of our journey, as we were paddling our canoes I happened to look up at this one pine tree, and there was a black bear lazily sitting high up in that tree. We all agreed that if we were traveling at a faster pace we wouldn't have seen him! I was thinking how often in our fast-paced world we miss the things God has for us. After we left the boundary waters we stopped for lunch. Doug took our group picture underneath the sign that welcomes people to the boundary waters. Before we left that spot to paddle back across Crane Lake, we split up into groups of two to pray for one another. Then on Saturday morning we had the opportunity to tell of our experiences to the Duluth congregation of the WCG, who had funded the trip. They also gave us T-shirts with the Servants' Passage logo on them. It's kind of cool to think about the fact that there are only twelve of them, and you can't get them unless you go on this trip. So there are only eleven of us in the world who have one of these, and one will be on display at future church events. One of the interesting things about this trip, though, was that I returned home with $500 more than I started with! Thanks for the gift — you know who you are!

With numberless blessings each moment He crowns,
And filled with His fullness divine,
I sing in my rapture, oh, glory to God!
For such a Redeemer as mine.
He hideth my soul in the cleft of the rock,
That shadows a dry, thirsty land;
He hideth my life in the depths of His love,
And covers me there with His hand,
And covers me there with His hand.

Peace and blessings to you!
Your friend in Christ
George Denn

August 19, 2006

———⊗⊗⊗———

Proverbs 20:24: *A man's steps are directed by the Lord. How then can anyone understand his own way?*

Last evening I was watching a movie on DVD with my dad and two sisters. The movie was "Oh God!" from 1977 starring George Burns and John Denver. That means I would have been fifteen years old when the movie was made. I find it very interesting how many of the old shows and movies I used to watch seem to contain some sort of spiritual lesson or message in them. I can really relate to the grocery store clerk Jerry Landers and how his life drastically changed the day God decided to "show up" and start doing something in his life! As I reflect on my own conversion experience, I remember how I was determined to be a millionaire before I was thirty, but as **Proverbs 16:1** states, *To man belong the plans of the heart, but from the Lord comes the reply of the tongue.* So instead I have to settle for being a poor guy at age forty-four! I never intended to be a follower or disciple of Jesus Christ either; as a matter of fact, I had no interest whatsoever! In my former way of viewing things, being a Christian would mean having to go to church all the time and pray all the time, and I figured that couldn't be any fun! Well, God had to adjust my way of thinking on all of that, sometimes using some pretty painful ways. I've probably read the book of Job more than any other book in the Bible, because whenever I've had a bad day or a hard time with things in my life I could always read about Job! I don't care who you are, I doubt you've had it worse than he did! Anyway, to sum things up in the simplest terms, my view of what a Christian is was **not correct**! I found out there is a whole other world of people to meet and things God has for you to do that I never knew existed.

John 6:44: Jesus said, *"No one can come to me unless the Father who sent me draws him, and I will raise him up at the last day."*

So for all of you who think like I did or who have a negative view of Christianity, all I can say is this: when God decides to show up in your life and you find Him to be real, you'll have fun!

It also never was my intention to write these stories, either. How it all got started was a lady by the name of Darlene Woods was looking for people to write stories for our church's newsletter called "The Tapestry". When I first saw the request in the church bulletin, I said to myself, *I don't think I will get involved with that*! Then when Darlene came up to me and asked if I would write an article for the paper, my response was, "I suppose I could, but I really don't know what I would write about!" I decided I would just write about my everyday walk with the Lord and the people I came into contact with on my walk. But what would I call the articles I wrote? At that time God had given me this slogan for my hay business: HAY BY GEORGE! So I just changed it to Hey, By George! as a way of saying hello from me to the reader. After a year or so the church newsletter was discontinued, so I just figured I would quit writing the stories, but Darlene encouraged me to keep writing them. So I just sort of started sending them to people via email and regular mail as a non-threatening way of evangelizing. In all the years I have sent them out, I have had only two people ask me to quit sending them, and I immediately granted their request. Several years went by and I found myself in a severe financial crisis, and I felt that my Christian witness had been destroyed and that probably no one was getting anything out of these stories anyway. So if God hadn't intervened, my story written for May 26, 2002, would have been the last one.

But God had other plans for my writing. A lady who was dying from cancer named Cheryl Hornick was sitting in the same pew as I was one Sunday at church, and she asked me if I was the person who wrote the *Hey By George!* stories. I told her that I was, and she said that she got so much out of them and really enjoyed them. That reason alone is why I started writing again! So because of Cheryl Hornick, who is no longer with us, I was able to write the stories beginning with the November 30, 2002, story and beyond, which is now the bulk of them! Also Robert Morris and Jim Hime helped type my stories and correct my very poor grammar.

So I really have to give Darlene Woods, Cheryl Hornick, Bob Morris, and Jim Hime all the credit, because if it had not been for these four good people, *Hey By George!* would not exist. Two years ago I started putting these stories in book form while working at one of my pumpkin stands in the fall. I gave away 143 copies that first year. A short time after the pumpkin season was over, I was wondering if maybe this was something God wanted me to continue doing. I was looking out my porch door as I was thinking this, and I noticed the mail carrier turning into my driveway. He delivered five pounds of pumpkin seeds that I had ordered and said that he had read my stories and really enjoyed them! So last year I put them out on all four of my pumpkin stands, and 500 copies were given away. So I really don't know who all reads them, but I do know that some of them have made it across the ocean, which is better than I have done! In these stories I have used Bible verses knowing that a lot of people don't really read the Bible. It also is not my intent to try to convince anyone of anything; I will let the Holy Spirit do that. I am only taking the Scriptures and trying to make them relevant to my everyday life, as well as how I interpret them and how I see God, Jesus Christ, and Holy Spirit — the triune God. I always pray before I write, and I am generally surprised in the direction I believe God takes me, because each story never seems to come out quite the way I imagined it would when I began writing it! I have come to see that God uses many people with different points of view to get His message across. It is my hope that I glorify God and not myself through these stories. I also want to thank all of you who were moved by the Holy Spirit to donate to get these stories published, for you are an answer to prayer! Last winter I asked God if He wanted these stories published, and that if He did, then He would have to supply the funds —which He did! So this will probably be the last story for this volume as once again autumn is upon me and time probably will not permit me until the harvest is over to write another, and then God willing I will submit this for publishing!

> **John 21:25:** *Jesus did many other things as well. If every one of them were written down, I suppose that even the whole world would not have room for the books that would be written.*

Peace and blessings to you all!
Your brother in Christ,
George Denn

If the Holy Spirit leads you to comment, I would appreciate hearing from you.

George Denn
59381 243rd Street
Kasota, MN 56050